Tribe

FIREFLY BOOKS

A FIREFLY BOOK

Published by Firefly Books Ltd. 2010

First printing

Publisher Cataloging-in-Publication Data (U.S.)
Gibbon, Piers.
  Tribe : endangered peoples around the world / Piers Gibbon.
[192] p. : col. photos. ; cm.
Includes index.
Summary: In words and pictures the culture, beliefs and environmental adaptations of over 200 indigenous peoples, from the barely contacted to those tribes whose identity has almost disappeared as it integrates into wider society.
ISBN-13: 978-1-55407-742-7
ISBN-10: 1-55407-742-7
1. Tribes -- Pictorial works. 2. Indigenous peoples -- Pictorial works. I. Title.
779/.93058 dc22   GN492.5G533   2010

Library and Archives Canada Cataloguing in Publication
Gibbon, Piers
  Tribe : endangered peoples around the world / Piers Gibbon.
Includes index.
ISBN-13: 978-1-55407-742-7
ISBN-10: 1-55407-742-7
  1. Indigenous peoples. I. Title.
GN380.G52 2010   305.8   C2010-900765-4

Published in the United States by
Firefly Books (U.S.) Inc.
P.O. Box 1338, Ellicott Station
Buffalo, New York 14205

Published in Canada by
Firefly Books Ltd.
66 Leek Crescent
Richmond Hill, Ontario L4B 1H1

Printed in China

Tribe

Endangered Peoples
Around the World

Piers Gibbon

WITH JANE HOUSTON

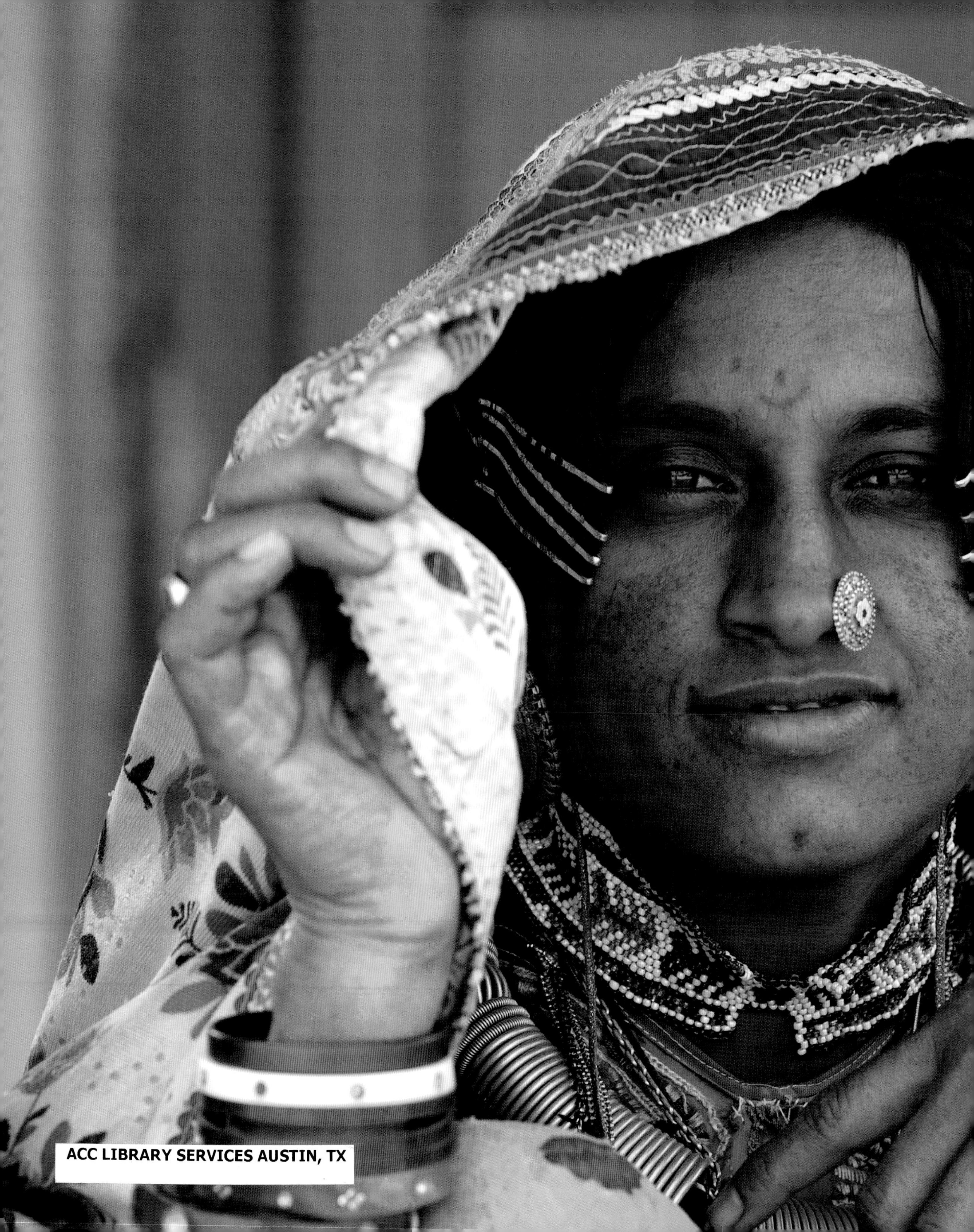

Introduction: A Savage History

The word "tribe" has a controversial history, but is now losing its negative connotations. A tribe is best defined by its members rather than by outsiders – a group of people can be said to belong to the same tribe if they regard themselves as having the same customs and language, if they are descended from the same group of ancestors, or if they have a sense of political affiliation that reaches beyond the family unit. The members of a tribe typically regard themselves as sharing a tribal name and a tribal territory – and what ends up being defined as a tribe is usually a number of smaller local communities. Many tribes simply refer to themselves as "people" in whatever language they speak.

At the start of the 21st century, at least 150 million people belong to tribes and take pride in their unique tribal identity and culture. This is not to romanticize their lives, which are often full of hardship. Tribal membership does not guarantee equality of opportunity for both sexes, for instance. And, just like national identity, tribal identity can lead to extreme violence, such as the massacres of the Rwandan Tutsis by the Hutus in 1994.

For many centuries, tribes have been the victims of colonialization. Recently, they have battled against armies, corporations, and nations for the rights to their land, their language, and even their children. They often struggle for survival. Yet across the globe, from the Kalahari Desert to the Amazonian rainforest, tribes live on in vibrant communities that are constantly adapting to a changing world. The diversity of humanity should surely be celebrated. Tribes should be celebrated. That is the purpose of this book.

Opposite: The endurance of tribal traditions such as facial tattooing is a declaration of pride in tribal identities that continues into the 21st century.

Different tribes for different people

Not all tribes fit academic definitions. The Amba of Uganda, for example, speak two totally different languages, but nevertheless regard themselves as one tribe. The Zuni of New Mexico are a tribe, but they live in just one *pueblo*, or village. In Kenya, the Dorobo are scattered among the Nandi and the Masai; they hunt and perform rituals with them, but regard themselves as an entirely separate tribe. As with any attempt to summarize the infinite variability of human behaviour, there are always arguments and controversies. The Amish in North America, with their traditional family and social structures, and strictly enforced lifestyle, fulfil perhaps all the criteria for definition as a tribe – yet this word is not used by them or by the outside world.

What's in a word?

The word "tribe" comes from the Latin *tribus*, which originally referred to any of the three divisions of the ancient Roman state – the Latins, Sabines, and Etruscans – and it is possible that these peoples were recognizable as tribes in the modern sense. However, when Julius Caesar reported Rome's conquests back from the frontiers in the 1st century BC, he never used *tribus* to describe what today would be defined as a tribe: he preferred *civitates* (states) and *nationes* (nations).

His writings also show an "us" and "them" division that foreshadows colonial attitudes to tribal life. Like other Roman authors, he wrote disparagingly about aspects he found particularly repellent, such as the practice of human sacrifice among the Celtic druids. In general, for these writers the Roman way of life was self-evidently modern, rational, and fair, and represented the future. Just occasionally, however, there was admiration for a tribe's overall bravery, or for some small aspect of its members' lives that could be regarded as being almost as good as the Roman way of doing things.

Since the time of the Roman Empire, "tribe" has had a chequered history. It has come to be regarded as an unhelpful concept, and in the latter part of the 20th century most anthropologists stopped using the word in academic works. Some felt that because it could not be precisely defined it was useless. Others found the term tainted by the colonial past. African scholars, in particular, felt that the term was insulting. Nonetheless, it is a popularly understood word, and one that looks set to be around for a while, especially when it is used to describe groups who have resisted much integration with the Western world. Today, "tribe" is usually replaced with "ethnic group" – especially when the different people who make up an industrialized society are discussed – or "indigenous

Opposite and below, clockwise from top left:
Tattooed Choco girl, Panama; Bakha hill-tribe
woman, Chiang Mai, Thailand; Hamar
tribeswoman, Ethiopia; Huaorani woman,
Amazon rainforest, Ecuador; Quechua man,
Peru; a Craja girl from the Brazilian Amazon;
Toposa boy, Sudan; Inuit man, Tasaliq,
Greenland; Woman from the Megwal tribe of the
Kutch, India; Kofure village woman, Papua New
Guinea; Apatani woman, India; Berber woman,
Morocco; Young Padaung girl, Thailand; Man
from the Kel Kummer Tuaregs, Sahara Desert;
Woman from the Gabada tribe, Orissa, India;
Karo tribesman, Ethiopia.

people". However, it would be good to think that we are headed for a post-colonial, post-exploitative world where "tribe" would be a word that is used with respect.

A brief history of tribes

The 150 million people who belong to tribes are equal to half the current population of the United States, and live in more than 60 countries: on the continents of Africa, Eurasia, and the Americas; on the islands of Melanesia; in the Arctic Circle and the Australian desert; and in countries as diverse as Russia, Peru, and the Philippines.

Isolated tribes

More than 100 indigenous tribes are thought to live in isolation from other people. Most of them live in Brazil, where FUNAI (the National Indian Foundation), the government agency responsible for indigenous people, claims there are at least 67 uncontacted groups in either Brazil or the countries on its north-western borders. West Papua (formerly Irian Jaya) is thought to have around 44 uncontacted groups, which makes it the country with the second largest number of isolated tribes.

For most of the 20th century, FUNAI (then known as the Indian Protection Service) actively sought to contact isolated tribes in an attempt to open the Amazon basin up to the world and employed expert explorers of the region to seek them out. It was a dangerous job. Malaria and other diseases are rife in the rainforest, and tribes often greeted outsiders with violence; many explorers were killed. The explorers' motto was, "Die if you must, but never kill", and they vowed never to react violently to the tribes they tracked

Contact with outsiders resulted in the deaths of thousands upon thousands of tribespeople, who had no immunity to Western infectious diseases.

The Pintupi Nine

Although the history of contact is often one of tragedy for tribes, there are also stories that celebrate the human capacity to survive life-changing events. An example is the Pintupi Nine, a nomadic aboriginal family of the Pintupi tribe of Western Australia, who came in from the desert in 1984. Warlinipirri and his family are said to be the last tribespeople who were unaware of the white man. They were hunting when Warlinipirri saw a camp fire in the distance and on approaching it – naked and carrying a spear – found an aboriginal family cooking a meal near a four-wheel drive van. They gave him the water he asked for, but the son, frightened by Warlinipirri's appearance, shot his rifle in the air and the Pintupi family fled into the remote parts of the Gibson Desert. The campers told the coordinator of the nearby community about their encounter, and a few days later, a search party of mainly aboriginal trackers discovered the family's camp and persuaded them to go to Kintore, about 250km (155 miles) away. From there they were driven another 27km (17 miles) to an aboriginal community where, to their huge surprise, they met members of their extended families.

Warlinipirri and his brothers and sisters were in their teens in 1984, and today most of them are artists. They make a considerable amount of money from their paintings, which they put towards supporting their network of relatives. One of the brothers, Yari Yari, went back to the desert in the mid-1980s, where he returned to the nomadic lifestyle of his youth.

The Tasaday: a Stone Age community?

The desire to see the Sentinelese as a direct link with our Stone Age past echoes the case of the Tasaday. When this tribe first appeared in the world's media, they were described as cave-dwellers in the Philippines, who had been undisturbed for over 1000 years until a hunter from a neighbouring tribe stumbled across them. Eventually, the hunter mentioned their existence to the government adviser on national minorities, a rich playboy called Elizalde. Elizalde flew into the rainforest to meet the Tasaday in June 1971. On hearing news of this gentle, peaceful tribe, who had no concept of violence, reporters and anthropologists flocked to visit them, and their story captivated the media. A few years later, the Filipino government ended access to the Tasaday, and forbade outsiders to visit them.

The next publicized encounter was in 1986. By then the government of the Philippines had changed, and a Swiss journalist found the Tasaday living in huts and wearing jeans and T-shirts. They told him (through a translator) that they had never lived in the caves and that Elizalde had instructed them to pose as a Stone Age tribe. Suddenly, questions were asked. Why had the Tasaday not become sick following contact with outsiders? Why were there no signs of burial places? How did they make tools without any knowledge of metallurgy? Ultimately, how could they have been isolated when they lived only a few miles from the nearest village? A theory developed that the Tasaday had been nothing more than an elaborate hoax on the part of Elizalde and his government allies, who had coerced local farmers into acting as fake hunter-gatherers. The world's media, slightly red-faced, turned their back on the tribe.

However, in the 1990s the group was studied by a researcher from the University of Hawaii, who concluded that their language was not fake, and was distinct from that of the nearby farmers. He speculated that the Tasaday were a splinter group from another local tribe, who had fled into the rainforest about 150 years ago, and did have some contact with neighbouring tribes. So they were not the romantic "Stone Age" community living in pristine isolation that had caught the world's imagination. But nor were they merely a hoax. The media had only ever described the tribe in sensationalist terms; the reality was more complicated.

down. However, contact with outsiders resulted in the deaths of thousands upon thousands of tribespeople throughout the region, who had no immunity to Western infectious diseases like flu, measles, and the common cold. Peoples such as the Matis of Brazil, who were first contacted in 1978, suffered from epidemics and many died; in the 1980s it was reported that there were not enough healthy Matis to bury the tribe's dead. For the past 20 years FUNAI has not attempted to contact isolated tribes; the current policy is simply to locate them, protect their lands, monitor them, and prevent outsiders encroaching on their territory.

Most uncontacted tribes in the Amazon basin are probably the descendants of people who fled the massacres caused by a rubber boom that lasted from 1879 to 1912. Slavers abducted tribesmen in the western Amazon and put them to work tapping rubber for the global market. The region rapidly became a nightmare of extreme brutality and bloody clashes between tribes and rubber tappers. Around 90 per cent of the indigenous population are thought to have died, and survivors fled deeper into the forest to escape the violence. It is easy to understand why the people descended from these refugees might choose to reject contact with the outside world.

The right of isolated tribes to live the way they have for millennia is enshrined in international law through the United Nations Declaration of Human Rights in 1948 and the International Labour Organization Conventions on Indigenous and Tribal People in 1957 and 1989. Sadly, this right is only sporadically honoured. The Akunsu tribe in Rondonia, Brazil, which was contacted in the 1990s, had only six surviving members little over a decade later. One of them reported that the tribe had been overrun by loggers who sent gunmen into its areas to drive it out.

The Sentinelese have remained one of the most isolated peoples in the world and little is known about their culture.

The group is expected to die out within a generation. In Colombia, a first contact in 2003 with the Nukaak Maku led to a mass outbreak of disease, as a result of which half its members died. The unexposed immune systems of isolated people mean that an entire tribe can be eradicated if one of its members meets an outsider who has what is a trivial infection in the industrialized world: a cold, a cough, or a slightly raised temperature.

A 60,000-year history

The Indian government, responding to international pressure, has decided not to force contact with the Sentinelese of the Andaman Islands in the Bay of Bengal. This tribe is thought to have descended from a population that has lived on the islands for up to 60,000 years. Outside contact with other Andaman tribes, the Onge and the Great Andamanese, led to disaster. In both cases, the populations crashed and the tribespeople now rely largely upon state hand-outs. The Sentinelese have remained one of the most isolated peoples in the world and little is known about their culture. However, they make tools from metal recovered from ships wrecked on their islands' reefs. Despite this, they are commonly described as "Stone Age" – a term that has angered many campaigners who believe it denigrates the achievements of tribal people – and the tribe is often presented as an example of man living in a natural, pristine state.

Saving souls

Article 8.1 of the 2007 United Nations Declaration on the Rights of Indigenous Peoples states: "Indigenous peoples and individuals have the right not to be subjected to forced assimilation or destruction of their culture." Recent stories of contact with isolated tribes show how necessary it is to uphold this right. In Paraguay, in 1979 and 1986, the American fundamentalist New Tribes Mission helped to organize "manhunts" where large groups of the Ayoreo–Totobiegosode tribes were forcibly brought out of the rainforest. Several tribespeople died during these encounters, and others later succumbed to disease.

At this time a number of religious groups were battling for the souls of the tens of thousands of indigenous people in Paraguay's Chaco, which had been penetrated by outsiders only in the previous decade. The groups included Mormons, Mennonites, Anglicans, Lutherans, 60 Americans from the New Tribes Mission, and Roman Catholic priests from the Franciscan, Oblate, Salesian, and Divine Word orders. The fundamentalists and Catholics took very different approaches to their work: the fundamentalists sought "unreached tribes" and the Catholics concentrated on helping communities that had been forced off their land.

Some Totobiegosode groups left the rainforest in 1998 and 2004; continual invasions of their land by ranchers meant that they constantly had to abandon their traditional homes. An unknown number still live a nomadic life in the forest, choosing to remain in isolation. Although they are protected by human rights law, the tribe faces constant and escalating threats from ranchers clearing the forest.

The stolen generations

The industrialized world often thinks it knows what is best for tribal cultures, and, in particular, for indigenous children – a stark illustration of the concept of "us" and "them". Us means "civilized" and "beneficial"; them equals "barbaric" and "harmful". Across the world there are examples of states and religions removing children from their families and tribes to be placed in institutions or with new, more "acceptable" families, often in an attempt to end the existence of an indigenous culture.

In Canada, the Indian Residential School System was founded in the 19th century to separate Native American children from their families and force them to be assimilated by European-Canadian society. They were placed in schools run by Christian denominations, and were sometimes punished for speaking their own languages or practising their own faiths. In 2008, the government of Canada issued an apology to the country's indigenous people: "The burden of this experience has been on your shoulders for far too long. The burden is properly ours as a government, and as a country. There is no place in Canada for the attitudes that inspired the Indian residential schools system to ever again prevail. ... The government of Canada sincerely apologizes and asks the forgiveness of the aboriginal peoples of this country for failing them so profoundly. We are sorry."

A controversial ecocampaign

In 2008, photographs taken from the air that showed tribespeople in a clearing in the rainforest on the Peru–Brazil border trying to scare off the aeroplane made front pages across the world as evidence of an undiscovered tribe. A few days later, a more nuanced story started to appear: that the tribe had been known about since 1910, and that the pictures were possibly part of an ecocampaign against encroachment into the forest by the timber and petroleum industries. The flyover to photograph the tribespeople was not a lucky accident, but was planned (using the thoroughly modern means of a Google Maps image that showed an interesting-looking clearing in the forest). The idea was to prove that the most iconic of human societies, "an uncontacted tribe", still existed in an area endangered by deforestation.

José Carlos Meirelles is a *sertanista* – an expert on indigenous tribes – and is employed by FUNAI. When the media storm had died down a bit, he admitted he had planned the publicity stunt in order to protect a tribe that was in danger of losing the territory in which it had thrived for countless years.

He said in an interview, "Alan García [the president of Peru] declared recently that the isolated Indians were a creation in the imagination of environmentalists and anthropologists – now we have the pictures...When I saw them painted red, I was satisfied, I was happy. Because painted red means they are ready for war, which to me says they are happy and healthy defending their territory."

This story shows that the media-saturated, ever-changing industrialized world is hungry for news of people living in a way that has hardly changed for centuries. It also shows that there is confusion about what is meant by "uncontacted". Charities like Survival International (*see* page 188) used the term to indicate that the tribespeople were isolated from other cultures in Peru and Brazil, but in general the media interpreted it as implying that the tribe was completely unknown. Perhaps the extent of the controversy surprised even Senor Meirelles.

Governments in many other countries, including Australia, have recognized the inhumane cruelty of assimilation policies. In 1997, Harald V of Norway apologized to the Sami peoples for "the injustice committed against the Sami people through the harsh policy of Norwegianization"; and New Zealand's government has apologized to three different Maori tribes for the impact of colonization.

Lessons from tribal societies

People living in tribal societies are starting to be regarded as something more than just novelties. For example, there is a certain wistfulness in the way some parenting manuals describe a tribal upbringing. Tribes offer more access to childcare, and are in many ways more "child centred" than Western communities. And there has been a recognition that, in the words of a proverb from the Yoruba of Nigeria: "It takes a village to raise a child."

There is a certain wistfulness in the way some parenting manuals describe a tribal upbringing.

"Babies, like puppies, played about beside the family fire without interference from their respective elders." The author of this quote, Jean Liedloff, is an American writer who spent 2½ years with the Yequana of Venezuela. In her best-selling book on child-rearing, *The Continuum Concept* (1975), she is full of praise for what she sees as the long-term benefits of allowing growing children to enjoy the maximum freedom and responsibility. However, she does accept that in the industrialized world, "Few could manage to allow the free playing with sharp knives and fire and the freedom of watersides that the Yequana permit".

Tribes are also seen to represent ecological hope for the future. "Only when the last tree has died and the last river been poisoned and the last fish been caught will we realize we cannot eat money" is a prophecy from the Cree tribe, an Algonquian-speaking people who lived historically from Minnesota westward. It has been quoted more than 1.9 million times online, usually as above, but occasionally with additional ecocrimes or with "will we realize" changed to "will the white man realize". This level of interest shows that the Cree prophecy strikes a chord with many people in the industrialized world.

Inherited knowledge

Tribal societies have crafted vital, often beautiful tools from the raw materials of the forest, the tundra, and the desert, from flint knives to poison-dart blowguns via fish traps and vessels for carrying water. They have kept warm by creating fire, and used that fire to preserve foods and smoke animal skins to make them waterproof. And they have learned how to make a musical instrument from a hunting bow, in order to amuse children by telling them how to use it to entice a deer close enough to kill it. Looking at the significance of the similarities and ancestral connections between these tools and skills and those of the 21st century is more interesting than just marvelling at their diversity. The industrialized world has improved on most of them. But without these first beginnings there would be nothing to improve upon. Indeed, tools made from skin, bone, wood, and fibre are sometimes still the best available on the planet, especially when the total environmental cost of production is taken into account.

The ability to inherit knowledge by transmitting information both in the group and down through the generations is the reason why humans are the dominant species on earth. Without this ability to communicate we would have remained a more or less successful type of African ape. Instead, the ultimate aim for people across the globe is to create healthy, happy, and stable communities within which

Next page top: A Masai man looks out from Lake Natron, a salt lake in Tanzania. Africa's Great Rift Valley has been home to hunter-gathering populations since the dawn of human evolution.

Next page below: Bahadur Shah, a Kashmiri nomad, drinks water from Kausar Nag Lake, high in the Himalayas. A nomadic life comes with challenges at altitudes of over 3000m (9850ft), where temperatures drop below freezing for months on end.

they are able to feed themselves and raise their children. And across the world, and over the centuries, tribal societies have invented an extraordinary range of ways in which to live from, and within, their environments. All of them are responses to the essential human question: how to survive and how to thrive.

What this book is about

The purpose of this book is to describe and celebrate the diversity and ingenuity of tribal cultures. In today's world, it appears that societies are increasingly homogeneous: anywhere on the globe it is possible to buy the same clothes, eat in restaurants that serve the same kind of food, and read the same fiction. Yet away from city streets, more than 150 million tribal people are living in a variety of environments, from icecaps to sweltering rainforests. Each tribe has its unique way of understanding, creating, and interacting with its surroundings. Learning how they do this enables us to appreciate the glorious variety of the world we live in, and better understand the strengths and flaws of our own social structures. The more we know about tribal peoples, the more the similarities between humans, no matter where they are, become apparent; and the prouder we can be of our world's ingenious tribal cultures. Sadly, the rights and lives of indigenous peoples are often marginalized, on both a national and an international stage; there are many examples of the exploitation of tribes and the loss of their cultures. By celebrating our common humanity, we can help to prevent the tragedy of cultural annihilation.

The book is organized by themes, and tribal cultures from across the world are compared in each chapter. Chapter 1 focuses on how and what tribal peoples eat and drink. It also provides information on hunting, gathering, farming, and fishing, and on the symbolic and social functions of food and drink. Chapter 2 looks at tribal dress and decoration, and shows how clothes are both functional and a means of expressing identity, allegiances, and notions of beauty. In Chapter 3, the homes of nomadic and settled tribes are described in terms of their architecture and symbolic importance. Chapter 4 discusses the different forms and meanings of love, sex, and marriage in tribes around the world. The ways in which tribal peoples relax, and the importance of storytelling, dance, jokes, art, and music are looked at in Chapter 5. Social organization is studied in Chapter 6, which describes how tribes establish laws, punish criminals, maintain peace, and participate in wars. Chapter 7 focuses on tribal beliefs, and examines myths, rituals, religions, and healthcare. Finally, the last chapter looks into the future of tribes in tomorrow's complicated and changing world.

Anthropological research and sources

Most of the information in the book is sourced from research by anthropologists. In the early 20th century they developed the method of participant observation to collect information about a tribe. This meant that anthropologists spent long periods, usually years, living with a tribe, or continually revisited the same people. During this time, they collected qualitative data about the tribe's culture by sharing in its daily life, observing its ceremonies and rituals, and questioning people in the community. Anthropologists often worked alone, but were sometimes accompanied by their partner or children, which could give them an even greater insight into various aspects of social life. After a period of study, the anthropologist wrote an ethnography about the tribe they had researched, in which they described and interpreted aspects of social life. Early classics in the genre include *Argonauts of the Western Pacific* (1940) by Bronislaw Malinowski and *The Nuer* (1940) by E E Evans-Pritchard. More recent ethnographies are *Spears of Twilight* (1996),

a study of the Achuar of the Amazon by Philippe Descola, and *We Share Walls* (2007), an ethnography of Berber Morocco by Katherine Hoffman.

The convention in ethnography – the branch of anthropology concerned with individual human societies – is to describe behaviour in the present tense. However, even though a description is in the present tense, it describes behaviour at the particular point in time at which it was observed by the ethnographer. This convention is followed in many sections of the book – for example, in the description of Nyakyusa boys' villages in Chapter 6.

Other sources for the information in the book are reports by journalists and missionaries, historical documents, government reports, non-governmental organization research, museum artefacts, tribespeople themselves, and the personal experiences of the author. It is important to remember that there is often no objective "truth" in descriptions of human behaviour and customs. Even if information comes from an indigenous "informant", it is possible they may want to conceal the truth or deliberately spread misinformation – to make the researcher look foolish, or simply as a joke. If a wedding ceremony in the West was reported by three different people – a family member, an anthropologist, and a journalist – it is unlikely they would all describe and interpret it in the same way. For this reason, descriptions in this book need to be seen as interpretations of tribal cultures rather than definitive accounts.

1 Food and Drink

A human can struggle to stay alive for more than a month without food – and is likely to die in just three days without water. But food does not only provide the nutrition and energy that keep us alive. It also has a cultural value. It can be a source of prestige and wealth. It is integral to courtship rituals across the world and is used to welcome guests. We can sacrifice food to gods or ancestors and break bread to establish friendships. Eating certain foods can be forbidden, or encouraged. And like all other animals, we must get what we need from our environment, whether we live in a desert, a rainforest, or a city.

Different tribes, different customs

Tribes get their sustenance in a variety of ways: through hunting and gathering; through cultivating crops; through keeping livestock; and through trade, barter, and exchange. What people eat and how they eat it also varies across the world, and whether a food is served raw or cooked, fresh or rotten depends not only on individual tastes but also on tribal traditions. The sourcing, preparation, and consumption of food and drink are highly cultural activities that fulfil a basic animal need. The following anthropological description of a

formal dinner party in the West is an example of just how specific these activities can be.

Hosts and guests sit in upright chairs around a table – sitting on the floor is wrong – and are served individual portions of food on china plates. They eat with metal tools held in a specific way rather than scooping up the food with their hands. The meal starts with something light and savoury, then there is a hot main course followed by a sweet dessert. The final food is often cheese, which may be so mouldy and rotten that it stinks. Fermented grape juice is served throughout the meal, and it is acceptable to become moderately intoxicated, though belching or slurping would be rude. Men and women sit side by side, even if their ages are different, and are expected to talk to each other while they eat. At the end of the meal it is customary to drink a caffeine-based stimulant.

Hunting and gathering

For the first two million years of human history we were hunters and gatherers. It is the life for which our bodies, our brains, and our social skills have evolved. Our ability to live in groups, to share food and resources, and to communicate effectively is what makes us the most efficient hunting and gathering animals on the planet. Hunter-gatherers adapted to travel across the world and they still survive in even the most inhospitable habitats.

What they eat is seasonal and varies hugely from tribe to tribe. Most hunter-gatherers rely mainly on plant foods for their calories, but small amounts of meat are a nutritional necessity. The Inuit of the Arctic are unusual in that their diet consists almost entirely of meat and fish. Only those who live far enough south to find berries have any vegetable

Previous page:
In Puttapakka village, Andhra Pradesh, India, women wait at a hand pump to fill their metal pots. Fetching water is an essential part of daily life for millions of people worldwide, and is usually a task carried out by women and children.

Opposite: Huli wigmen gut a wild pig in the Southern Highlands of Papua New Guinea. The Huli grow some crops, but a substantial part of their diet comes from hunting and gathering. The pig will provide valuable protein.

Right: In the Kalahari Desert, all liquid is precious, and it is necessary to use inventive methods of hydration. Here a G/wi child in Botswana's Ghanzi district drinks juices squeezed from pulped plants.

component in their food and, as a result, the Inuit often suffer from health problems, such as liver complaints, related to excessive vitamin A consumption. With this exception, most hunter-gather diets are high in nutrients; in fact, the switch to farming arguably led to worse nutrition and a decrease in health for people across the world.

Bush meat and insects

Through necessity, many hunter-gatherers have a broad diet and obtain energy and nutrition from lizards, snakes, and insects. Some tribes of the north-western Amazon region are reported to eat the lice they find in their hair when they groom themselves. In central Australia, the Arunta (gatherers who move from one place to another according to the seasons) use boomerangs and spears to catch kangaroos, wallabies, and emu. Any meat that goes off and turns green can be made edible again by soaking it in running water for two days, then cooking it – a process that kills any bacteria. This diet is supplemented with rats, lizards, grass seeds, tubers and fruits, and many insects.

Locusts, although a plague for agriculturists, are a gift from above for gatherers.

Locusts, although a plague for agriculturists, are a gift from above for gatherers. They are a nutritious food, and groups like the San of the Kalahari Desert in southern Africa make large fires in order to attract and collect them. The Berber of the Sahara roast locusts in earth fires built in the ground, then pound and pulverize them or eat them whole; they are said to taste like crayfish.

The Azande of north central Africa catch termites by enfolding the insects' mound with several layers of the broad leaves of a wood reed and creating a bulge in the wrapping. All the termites swarm into the bulge and are easily scooped out. Alternatively, the nests are dug up and the insects are harvested – the huge, fat queens are a particular delicacy. Termites can be roasted and eaten.

Sweet energy

Honey is a precious source of energy for hunter-gatherers, and a welcome treat. The San smoke bees out of trees, rocks, and holes, and use special hooks to remove the honeycombs. Sometimes they detect from a bee's flight that it is laden with nectar – it is lower in the air and flies more slowly than normal – and follow it to the honey. Alternatively, they may follow a honeybird to the nest; if so, they always give it a piece of the comb to thank it for showing them the way.

Below: Hadzabe'e hunter-gatherers collect honey from the branch of a tree, Lake Eyasi, Tanzania. The honeybird plays such a valuable role in the life of the tribe that it has a place in Hadzabe'e mythology.

Witchetty grubs and ghost moths

Witchetty grubs are eaten across most of Australia. The term is used to describe the large, white larvae of the cossid moth in particular, but also the grubs of other moths, such as ghost moths, and longhorn beetles. Cossid larvae live in the roots of acacias, from which they are extracted with a hooked stick. When cooked, they taste like scrambled eggs. The Pitjantjatjara of the central Australian desert catch large, white wood grubs, which have a taste similar to that of roast pork.

Large ghost moths are a traditional food for many southern Australian tribes, and typically emerge in the late afternoon after the first autumn rains have fallen. Huge fires are built to collect them – as they flutter towards the flames they are caught in nets – and they are then roasted. The coastal-living Wirrangu are among the people who dig for the moths' grubs and pupae. These are buried 1.2–1.8m (4–6ft) underground at the end of silk-lined tunnels that are found underneath cracks in the ground, especially over lateral tree roots, where the earth has fissured and contracted during dry weather. If the tunnels have been made recently, the linings are damp with a pungent smell, and the gatherer continues digging until he reaches the grubs. They are then cooked in ashes. As collecting them involves so much labour, they are considered a real luxury; their taste has been compared to that of warm cream and the crackling on roast pork.

Above: Witchetty grubs, extracted here from roots, are high in protein and are a prized source of nutrition in the outback, where they have been part of the aboriginal diet for centuries. The larvae often appear in traditional paintings and witchetty grubs are totem animals for some aboriginal clans (see page 32).

Hunting and fishing technology

Hunting animals requires sophisticated technology. Traps are found across the world, and vary from the spring snare of the African bush to the baited snares used across North America to trap large animals like bears. In Papua New Guinea, forest mammals such as pigs are caught with the stepped bait release snare. Many Amazonian tribes catch monkeys with spear traps.

Like hunting, fishing has a varied and sophisticated technology. Fish can be caught with traps woven from twigs, nets woven from bark and plant fibres, hooks made of bone, wood, and thorns, and by creating artificial flies as lures. Trout can be tickled out of the water and caught by hand.

Clockwise from left: Men balance on posts above shallow water to fish for herring in the Laccadive Sea, near Matara, Sri Lanka; A trapped kingfisher in the Nalbari district of Assam. Although hunting birds is banned in north-east India, where their populations are dwindling, local people continue to use them for food and medicine; A San man in the Kalahari Desert in Namibia sets a snare for guinea fowl; Woven baskets are used to trap fish in rivers all over the world, from the Amazon to the Nile and the Ganges. Here a Hambuskushu woman, with her child on her back, fishes

Toxic technology

Many hunting tribes use poison to kill their prey or to make it unconscious. The Masarwa San of the northern Kalahari put snake venom and the entrails of the noxious *n'gwa* caterpillar on their arrows for shooting animals such as gemsbok.

In the Amazon region, poison is used to stun fish in the water so that they rise to the surface where they can easily be collected by hand.

In forest environments, blowguns are the technology of choice for transporting poisons as they allow great precision over short distances. In Malaysia, the *sumpitan* is drilled out of a single ironwood branch. The huge investment in time and skill this requires – as well as the blowgun's effectiveness in putting meat in the cooking pot – makes it highly valuable. Three North American tribes – the Muskhogeans, Atticapas, and Chetimachas – took the blowgun to another level of sophistication by binding bundles of reeds together to make a "blowgun revolver" that enabled hunters to blow several darts in rapid succession. In the days of tribal warfare, the Punan tribe in the remote Malinau watershed in Indonesian Borneo used king cobra venom for their blowguns. In South America, the Choco people of western Colombia put the highly potent toxin secreted in the skin of the golden poison-dart frog (*Phyllobates terribilis*) on their darts. Many poisons are harmful to humans as well as their prey, and in such cases hunters are careful to cut out the affected meat. An exception is *curare*. This is used by many South American tribes, such as the Matses and Shuar, and could be regarded as the "perfect poison" because it is toxic only when it gets into the bloodstream – for example, as the result of an arrow wound. It is obtained from the bark of certain tropical trees, and is a muscle relaxant so potent that it stops respiration and leads to death. In the early 19th century, the British explorer Charles Waterton described *curare*'s fearsome powers. An Arawak Indian guide told him how a hunter "took a poisoned arrow and sent it at a monkey in a tree above him ... the arrow missed ... and in the descent struck him in the arm ... 'I shall never' said he 'bend this bow again'. And having said that, he took off his little bamboo poison-box, which hung across his shoulder, he laid himself down close by them, bid his companion farewell, and never spoke more." The lethal injections used when death sentences are carried out in the United States contain pancuronium bromide, a derivative of *curare*.

In forest environments, blowguns are the technology of choice for transporting poisons as they allow great precision over short distances.

Right: In the Namibian Kalahari Desert, a San hunter applies poison to the shaft of an arrow by carefully squeezing the toxins from a chrysalis on to a spot just beneath the arrow tip.

Next page left: A Kaluli man in Papua New Guinea hunts with a poisoned dart – an effective weapon in a forest environment where it is possible to stalk prey at close quarters.

Next page right: The Penan of the Borneo rainforest use poisoned darts in blowguns. Considerable skill is needed to hunt with the deadly accuracy necessary for a kill.

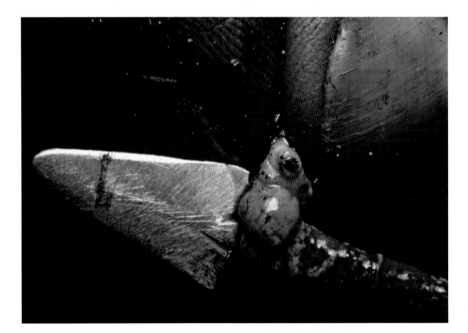

Communication and cooperation

Humans hunt more successfully when they work together than when they work alone. Our communication skills are thought to have arisen partly so that we could hunt efficiently in packs. The Warramunga of central Australia even have a sign language so that they can silently communicate the type of food they have seen to their companions. A curled, pointed finger shows that they have found a honeycomb by following bees to their nest, whereas a loose fist indicates that they have spotted a witchetty grub.

The Twa or Batwa pygmies of Uganda hunt gazelles and antelope with nets. One method is for the men to hang these from low branches so that they form a circle. When the circle is complete, some men move into it and make enough noise to frighten their prey into taking flight. The remaining men, and the women, guard the nets to make sure that once the animals have become entangled in them they cannot escape.

Man eaters

Throughout history some human beings have eaten the flesh of other members of our species. Shipwrecked sailors have had to do this in order to survive: early in the 19th century there were reports of cannibalism when a French frigate, the *Medusa*, ran aground off the West African coast and survivors on a raft were forced to eat the flesh of their dead companions. In 1972, passengers who escaped death when a plane crashed in the Andes resorted to cannibalism. There is something of a myth about tribal cannibalism, started by colourful reports of the practice in the Americas, written by European explorers and missionaries. And the explorer and journalist H M Stanley claimed that in Africa he captured cannibals who stank of human meat. However, as the anthropologist W Arens pointed out in *The Man-Eating Myth*, these 19th-century (and even 20th-century) accounts relied on hearsay rather than eyewitnesses. Today, although it is generally accepted that cannibalism among tribes has been wildly exaggerated, many anthropologists believe that man eating man was part of a ritual in some societies, rather than a desperate act.

Certainly, there is documented evidence that people consume parts of each other during funerary rites. Human flesh has limited nutritional value – it could provide emergency calories and protein, but unlike animal meats, poultry, and fish, it is almost totally lacking in vitamin B, so eating it is likely to be ritually rather than nutritionally important. The Yanomano of Venezuela consume the ashes of their deceased loved ones as a way of honouring the dead. In Brazil, the Wari practised cannibalism until as recently as the 1960s. Studies show they had different motives for this, ranging from respect when human flesh was eaten at funerals, to hate and anger when enemies were consumed during wars. Wari elders have told anthropologists that they cannot understand why outsiders are obsessed with the fact that they eat parts of a dead body, as this is only one part of a funeral ritual.

In 17th-century Europe, the use of medicines made from blood and parts of the human body was widespread. Fresh blood was thought to cure epilepsy and diseases including arthritis, reproductive problems, sciatica, warts, and skin blemishes were treated with various body parts. For example,

Many anthropologists believe that man eating man was part of a ritual in some societies, rather than a desperate act.

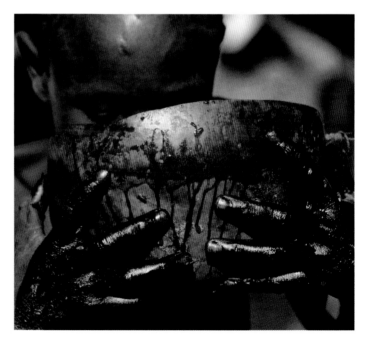

Below: A young Surma tribesman drinks cattle blood in Kormu, Ethiopia. The Surma believe that raw blood is a source of great strength for young warriors – a belief that is supported by the fact that blood provides iron, vitamins, and erythrin, an antibiotic.

the treatment for boils was to pass a dead man's hand – ideally still attached to the corpse – over the afflicted area seven or nine times over the course of three days. The bodies of executed criminals were a primary source for this type of material.

Farmers and agriculturalists

The first settled communities were established some 9000 years ago, in the valley of the Tigris and Euphrates rivers, and along the banks of the Nile. It is possible that finding a favourite vegetable or medicinal plant growing in a site that had previously been inhabited (especially in a rubbish tip or midden) was the spark that led to the deliberate sowing and growing of crops. Since then, agriculture and keeping livestock has allowed humans to regulate and plan their environment so that they can manage the food available to them. An example is the Mien, a hill tribe of the northern regions of Thailand, Laos, and Vietnam, who live on thickly forested slopes and practise swidden cultivation – a shifting field system in which a patch of land is cleared and burned, used for crops, and then left fallow for 10 years to recover. The Mien consider rice to be a source of life and strength, and serve it with every meal.

Below: A Berber woman from the lower Rif plains of Morocco bakes bread outdoors.

Below right: A Berber man oversees the drying of the fruit of the argan tree on a Moroccan rooftop. Argan oil, which is used as a dip for bread, is rare as the tree is endemic to Morocco and grows only in a small area.

Berber breads

The rural population of North Africa relies heavily on cereals. In the upper Atlas Mountains, the Ait Mgun Berbers cultivate barley, corn, millet, and wheat at high altitudes. These are boiled, eaten as couscous, or used for breads. A large, flat, round loaf eaten on feast days is made with wheat or barley, and is leavened with yeast. Making it is time consuming. The cereal is cleaned and separated, then pounded, winnowed, washed, and sieved. Next, it is kneaded with water, left to ferment, shaped, and baked. The process takes a total of 2½ hours, and creates six to eight loaves. Each adult is expected to eat about 150g (5oz) of bread, which is usually served with a tagine – a spicy stew – or sauce. Two other breads are made more quickly: "bread from the hearth", a thick, leavened bread cooked over hot coals, and "pan bread", an unleavened biscuit.

"Banana" bread

In south-west Ethiopia the Gurage eat the root and inner layers of the stem of the *ensete* – false banana plant – which are chopped, minced, and kneaded into a fibrous pulp comparable to unripened mashed yams. This is buried in an earth pit to ferment, a process that can take from two months to two years. The pit emits a foul smell, especially when it is opened to remove the fermented pulp, which is kneaded, shaped into a loaf, and pan-fried to make a bread called *wusa*. A staple of the Gurage diet, *wusa* is eaten with small servings of other foods such as beef, lamb, kale, or lentils. For festive occasions, it is made with the finest *ensete* and served on dried leaves of the plant, which are cut into plates, along with drinks such as barley beer, coffee with salt, spiced butter, or mead. For weddings or circumcision ceremonies, the meat of a freshly slaughtered bull is the centrepiece of the meal. It is customary to eat the flesh raw, dipping it in red pepper and washing it down with barley beer.

The *ensete* is a multipurpose plant. Its bark is used to insulate houses, it is burned as fuel, its root provides a medicine, and its fibres are sold to make rope and sacking. The number of plants in a man's garden – and their height and girth – is a mark of his standing in the community.

Sharing to survive

Some farming tribes, such as the Iteso of western Kenya, blend agriculture with hunting or gathering. Anthropologists Ivan and Patricia Karp worked with the Iteso and discovered

Below and left: A woman from the Omo River region of Ethiopia shaves and prepares the leaf and stem of a false banana plant. Following fermentation, the pulp is used to make *wusa* bread – a staple of the local diet.

that they always share food; even with the security provided by a mixed strategy of farming and foraging, procuring enough to eat can be difficult, and sharing helps to minimize the risk of hunger.

For the Iteso, the term "epog" is a huge insult. It is roughly translated as "self-sufficient" and refers to someone who feels that they have no obligation to share food; a greedy, foolish person who would eat secretly in a dark hut. The insult attached to the term shows how Iteso culture has adapted to an uncertain environment, in which it is necessary and sensible to build up a reciprocation network in order to survive.

The Iteso always eat communally. Unexpected visitors are welcomed, and children are fed wherever they happen to be when food is served. A meal always consists of a starch, usually a doughy mix made with cassava or sorghum – without this, it is not a meal – and meat or a relish of boiled vegetables. Only women are allowed to cook the starch, and this should be done on the woman's fireplace inside the home. Men are allowed to cook meat, but must do so outside and only by roasting it, never by boiling, which is how it is prepared by women.

Even the simplest meal means a vast amount of work for the women. They procure the food, collect firewood, and visit the local stream a couple of times every day for water; they carry the vessels for the water on their heads. Berries are considered to be children's food – only they find, and eat, them. It is also regarded as appropriate for children to collect insects. Rain brings out a myriad flying white ants, and the children pick hundreds of them out of the air, stuffing them into tins. The women then fry the insects in ghee to make snacks.

Village relationships

The Mambila in West Africa usually produce a surplus of maize and Guinea corn, and villages compete to give impressive gifts of food to each other, which establishes relationships between communities and reduces the risk posed by a low harvest. At the age of about 16, a boy chooses a gift partner, a boy of his own age, usually from a neighbouring village. The partnership is established by the offer, and acceptance, of beer. A pot of 18–22 litres (4–5 gallons) is shared by the boys and their friends, and is a sign of friendship and a signal that the partners will be welcome in each other's villages, and that friendly relations will be maintained between the communities. Each beermate makes a small contribution to the payment a groom makes to his bride's family, and each partner can be intimate with the other's wives. They are expected to help each other build their houses and when one of them dies the survivor must attend his funeral. Throughout their lives they offer each other presents of beer, particularly at feasts. Their villages also celebrate their partnership with gifts of food and beer in their names, even if neither of the partners is present.

Water: the source of life

Water is as essential to our survival as food, and hunter-gatherers are ingenious in their use of the natural environment to transport it from streams, lakes, or rivers to where it is needed. In New Zealand, the Maori hunted moas – ostrich-like, flightless birds native to the country that have been officially extinct for 200 years – and used their eggs as water carriers. The San of the Kalahari Desert in southern Africa still use ostrich eggs for this purpose.

In the 18th and 19th centuries, the Comanche, a Native American tribe that roamed the southern Great Plains of North America, transported water in carriers made from the stomachs of buffalo; these animals also provided them with skins that were used for clothing and tepee material, and the meat that was their staple food.

Ritual drinking

That drinking is often a highly ritualized event is apparent to anyone who has ever taken part in a wine-tasting session, enjoyed a coffee in Milan, or had afternoon tea in England. In many tribal cultures in the Amazon basin, people start

their day by drinking a powerful emetic that makes them vomit. For the Achuar of the Peruvian rainforest, this is *wayus*, an infusion of the leaves of various Aquifoliaceae plants. It is a bitter drink with a high level of caffeine, and Achuar households wake at about 3am to drink it and discuss the business of the day ahead. Traditionally, only men drank *wayus*, but today women use it as well. The caffeine makes it a powerful stimulant and the drink also acts as a purgative. Vomiting reduces the number of internal parasites that are endemic among Amazonian tribes and is symbolically cleansing, allowing the Achuar to begin each day feeling clean inside and ready for the day ahead.

Alcohol: a worldwide relaxant

Drinking fermented liquid and getting intoxicated is as much a pastime in tribal areas as it is in the cities of the United States or the villages of northern Europe. In the Amazon basin, tribes make a brew with manioc, which they chew up and then spit into water where it ferments. Among the Ashaninka this is known as *masato*, though it goes under many other names throughout the region.

The Lele of the Congo fill calabashes with palm wine that they drink in the evening. Sap is tapped from a mature palm, preferably one that is not old and rotting, and the micro-organisms it contains usually convert it into wine by the end of the day. The men are responsible for making the wine, whereas providing water is the task of the women. A typical adult drinks more wine than water, though the Lele dislike permanent drunkenness as much as they abhor excessive sobriety. As in many parts of the West, drinking alcohol is associated with relaxation; it is unusual for anyone to drink palm wine during the day, when the serious tasks of farming, hunting, weaving, and house building are done. Lele men meet in the *mapalu*, a small cleared area of forest or savannah in front of their village. Here they share the palm wine and discuss the community's affairs. Certain rules must be obeyed: the men cannot stand, but must sit or kneel; they must drink all the contents of a folded leaf or beaker at once, without sipping; and the oldest men must be served first. Drunkenness is met with disapproval as it is seen as the mark of a greedy man who has taken more than his fair share of the wine. Slight intoxication is tolerated in men, but not in women, who drink a "soft" (less alcoholic) version of the wine, and remain inside the village, staying sober.

Ceremonial meals

For many tribes, feasting at the end of the yearly harvest not only helps to establish alliances between villages but also maintains the status system and brings people together in communal celebrations. It is usual for the senior men to instruct their juniors to make alcoholic beer for the feast, and the entire village donates grain for this, along with labour and animals for meat. Food also plays an important role in rites of passage, such as marriage and initiation.

The Tiv of Nigeria cook chicken in a sesame-flavoured sauce to celebrate a man welcoming his first wife to his home. The chicken must be caught by the groom or his age mates – men who were initiated into adulthood at the same time as him – and the ingredients for the sauce are provided by his mother and her husband's other wives. The married men in the groom's family are responsible for cooking the chicken, so that everyone in the homestead is involved in preparing the meal.

Among the Avatime of the Togo hills in Ghana, meals are eaten throughout a cycle of ceremonies that celebrates a girl becoming a woman. Before she attends

Above: A woman of the Bonda tribe, Orissa, India, drinks sugar palm alcohol from a small gourd.

Opposite centre: The Maria tribespeople in the hills of Chhattisgarh state, India, use leaf cups to serve alcohol distilled from the mahuwa tree.

Opposite right: A G/wi woman of the Kalahari Desert drinks water from an ostrich egg. The G/wi often use ostrich eggs to store water during the rainy season and bury them in remote desert locations to be retrieved during the dry months.

The Tonga see a symbolically important link between humans and bees: both are social animals that live and work in cooperative groups.

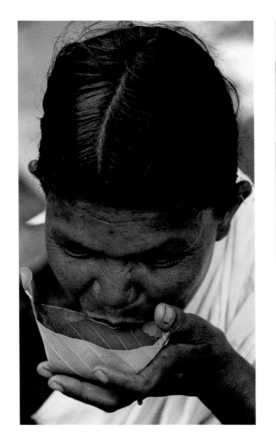

her initiation, a feast of green leaf stew, eggs, and rice flour porridge is prepared. Some of this goes to the local Avatime priests, who may also be given some bush meat, and the rest is eaten by postmenopausal women. No pepper is added to the stew as it is thought this irritant could negatively affect the relationship between the girl and her future spouse if it is eaten when her initiation is being celebrated. Days later, another batch of stew is cooked, this time for the children of the village. They wolf it down, after which water is poured over their hands, collected in a bowl, and given to the girl, who drinks it as one of the rituals performed during the ceremonial cycle.

The Yoruba of Nigeria use social occasions to show their status and generosity. Yam is their staple food, and is also regarded as a desirable prestige vegetable. It is always served socially, but in private families may eat other foods such as cassava, taro, or maize. Yams can be boiled, mashed, or made into fritters, flour, or porridge. They can also be made into a loaf, which is always served with a stew. The Yoruba are discerning eaters of yam and are very critical if it is not prepared to their taste. A man of position always has a pot of stew in his house to share with any visitors.

A man's wife is expected to learn and prepare her husband's favourite dishes. If a man is single this is his mother's task, or he asks a woman in his compound to cook for him. Men do not prepare their own food for fear of ridicule.

Symbolic consumption

Eating can be a highly symbolic act. Anthropologist Simon Charsley investigated the symbolism of the food served at traditional weddings in Glasgow, Scotland. When he asked what the cake represented, most people either had no idea what it stood for or said it it didn't stand for anything. His own guesswork is much more vivid: he suggests the white wedding cake could represent the body of the virginal bride, which is symbolically penetrated with a cake knife.

Courtship and eating

Just as a dinner date is part of courtship in the West, hunter-gatherers use food to attract potential partners. The Siriono of the eastern Bolivian lowlands live in an area where food is scarce and men use game to seduce their current and future wives, and to have affairs. However, in the Trobriand Islands, south-east of New Guinea, it is inappropriate for a man and woman to eat together until their relationship is considered to be serious. In fact, a couple enjoying a meal of yams in public is the first sign that they are married.

Food and gender

Food is linked to gender, in both its procurement and its preparation. Men most often hunt and women generally gather – and provide most of the food. Women normally fetch water and men are more likely to consume alcohol and

drugs. Certain foods are also associated with gender. For the Wamirans in Papua New Guinea, taro plants represent men's "children", and the number they own indicates their status and virility. But men cannot grow taro by themselves, and it is the task of women to plant and weed it, so a wife helps her husband to create his status. Conversely, the men of the Kalauna of Goodenough Island off the coast of Papua New Guinea establish their paternity by feeding their pregnant wives, which is seen as nurturing the foetus.

The Mehinaku of the Amazon region use food in female rites of passage. When a girl first menstruates, she must avoid eating fish because it is thought to be too full of blood. This food avoidance is symbolically ended when she eats, and spits out, a small bit of fish, a sign that she has reached adulthood. Sambia men in Papua New Guinea eat white sap to replenish their semen. The belief is that the foetus's skin and bone are provided by the father's semen, and its blood comes from the mother.

The Padhola of south-east Uganda use the cowpea plant to make a relish, *magira*, which is so sustaining that it must be eaten by a woman after the birth of her first boy and when her first girl is born. The growth of these plants is linked with wellbeing and the fertility of all living things. Their first flowering is the time for spring-cleaning, and homes are cleansed by throwing the ashes from hearths into the bush. This is when women hold fertility rituals, which also serve as a form of sex education for young girls.

Foods and taboos

Across the world there are dietary laws that prohibit people from eating certain foods. People belonging to religious groups, for example Jews, Muslims, and Rastafarians, are not allowed to eat pork. Similarly, tribes have forbidden foods.

The majority of tribes in Australia are organized into clans, each of which is represented by an ancestral totem, usually an animal. For most groups of aboriginal Australians eating the animal is forbidden, and is considered to be akin to consuming their ancestors. However, the prohibition is not absolute as it is sometimes essential to eat the animal in order to perform certain rituals. Among the tribes of central Australia, men who belong to a clan whose totem is the witchetty grub eat a few of the grubs during male initiation rites, which is thought to increase the witchetty population. But they never eat the chatunga bird as it is the totem of the clan from which they expect to take marriage partners.

The Tonga of the Zambezi valley have taboos about honey. During the initial period of marriage, a groom must not eat it with his bride until a year after they have had their first child. The bride can eat honey only at her father's house, and her husband may eat it only in the bush, after which he must wash his hands and face so that his bride cannot detect his secret snack. This is because the Tonga see a symbolically important link between humans and bees: both are social animals that live and work in cooperative groups. They are concerned that, just as the bee will flee the hive, a wife will flee her own nest if she has not become established there, so they seek to avoid reminding her of her potential transience.

As well as *magira*, the Padhola also make bird and fish relishes. These are luxuries that are often forbidden to women and children, and are reserved for men as signs of social standing and prestige. Pregnant women are not allowed to drink milk as it resembles semen and may turn a child white.

The Trumai of the Upper Xingu, a tributary of the Amazon, prohibit women from eating fish paste if they have just had a baby or are menstruating; anyone who is associated with producing blood is forbidden to eat fish. For this reason, a man is not allowed to eat fish paste if his wife has just undergone childbirth, or if he has recently killed someone. Women can eat fish while they are pregnant – because they stop bleeding – but are forbidden to eat meat, which is considered to be bad for the child.

Tribal cooking techniques

While tribes in many parts of the world grill or roast their fish or meat, those who live in colder regions rely primarily on boiling. The Inuit of the Arctic use sea water, fresh water, or a combination of the two to boil seal meat, their staple food. Blubber is added to the stock as a flavouring, and both the resulting broth and the meat are eaten. Cold seal meat is said to be particularly good with pickles, and seal liver is considered a delicacy.

The men of the Wola tribe in Papua New Guinea make an earth oven rather than using an open fire. After hunting they gather to dig a pit, and make a fire close to it to heat some stones. They line the pit with banana or other leaves and put in the hot stones, then add the meat of their prey (usually pork) and vegetables (such as sweet potatoes or onions). The pit is sealed with leaves, and hot stones are placed on top; water can be added to steam the food. Cooking takes a couple of hours, during which tasty morsels of meat may be roasted over the embers of the fire. When the pit is opened, the men take parcels of the food home to share it with their families. In the Vaupes region of Colombia, the Barasana use a technique

Above: Yapese men grill turtle meat on Satawal Island, Micronesia. Many marine conservationists are concerned about traditional hunting, but others argue that tribes have fished and hunted sustainably for hundreds of years (*see* The People of the Whale, page 181).

Opposite: A Mentawai hunter in Sumatra, Indonesia, spit-roasts a pig that he has caught.

that is part smoking and part grilling to prepare fish and meat as well as frogs, ants, caterpillars, beetle larvae, and chilli peppers. First, they make a smoking rack by balancing a wood frame, on two wooden supports, above a fire. Fish are usually smoked whole without gutting, and are generally laid flat on the rack. Alternatively, long sticks are threaded through their eyes and they are hung in rows; frogs are skewered through their jaws. Small fish take six hours to cook, bigger ones more than a day. Large chunks of meat require a big fire with the rack fairly high off the ground, and take up to three or four days and nights. For this reason they cannot be too big as they will rot in the middle while they cook.

If the food is to be stored, it is left on the rack until it is dry and brittle, but if it is to be eaten immediately, it is removed when it is still tender. The Barasana eat smoked meat with cassava and a condiment made from smoked chilli peppers and salt pounded in a mortar. Food that has been stored is soaked in cold water, then boiled in water with smoked chilli. The resulting stew is served with bread made from cassava.

The ways in which food and drink are prepared and enjoyed are as diverse as the cultural traditions of the world's societies and tribes. What they have in common is that eating and drinking are activities that both fulfil our basic needs and lead to emotional satisfaction.

2 Dress and Adornment

There is a crucial difference between clothing and ornament: clothing serves as protection from the elements and as a way of protecting our modesty, but it also developed from a desire to ornament the body. Archaeology and history show that even before we developed the concept of clothing we always tried to make ourselves attractive by using objects from the environment that attract the eye – bright and colourful decorations in the hair, strung around the neck, or looped across the stomach. It would be a mistake to assume that humans are entirely practical in their choices. Ornament satisfies a more elusive but just as important aesthetic value, and it will often win over protection or comfort.

Covering our nakedness

Humans are the only naked apes. Unlike the other, furrier primates, the hair on our heads grows extraordinarily long compared with the invisible downy hair over most of our body. We also have hair in the armpits and groin, which serves both to protect us and to trap bodily scent, which may give off a sexual signal to potential mates. Men exhibit the secondary sexual characteristic of growing hair on their jaw, and some, particularly those from groups that have evolved in colder climates, have coarse, wiry hair on their chests and backs. But the bodily hair of even the most hirsute of men doesn't compare with that of the gorilla, chimp, or orangutan. Our smoothness suggests that we evolved for a warm climate and indeed this is consistent with the evidence that almost the entire drama of hominid evolution was played out on an African stage. However, even Africa can be cool at night, so perhaps the earliest humans used skins and furs as protection when temperatures fell.

Walking upright is also thought to be a reason for our nakedness. Being bipedal means that we don't have to protect our whole bodies from the strength of the sun. Only the tops of our heads and our shoulders are exposed to glaring solar rays – hence our ability to grow longer hair on our heads in order to cover parts of the body most vulnerable to sunburn. So when and why did we start wearing clothes?

The origin of clothing

Professor Mark Stoneking and his team at the Max Planck Institute for Evolutionary Anthropology in Leipzig have carried out some revolutionary research, the results of which were published in the journal *Current Biology* in 2003. Instead of looking at fibres and other remains, the team analysed head and body lice gene sequences and variations in the genetic make-up of parasites. "When humans began to make frequent use of clothing, head lice moved into clothing and evolved as body lice," explained Professor Stoneking. By working out when this evolution took place, the team arrived at an approximate date for when our ancestors first began wearing furs and skins – around 72,000 years ago, much earlier than was previously thought.

Previous page:
Masai women at the opening of a new village are clothed in beautifully coloured wraps known as *kanga*.

Opposite: Akeme tribesmen and boys wear orange and white stripes of body paint at a sing-sing festival in Mount Hagen, Papua New Guinea.

Right: Two Ashanti noblemen in Kumasi, Ghana, wear elaborately woven kente cloth robes at a thanksgiving celebration in honour of the new *asantaheni* (Ashanti chief).

Material world

The next step occurred when humans first worked out how to turn plant fibres into cords. These cords were obviously very useful for all sorts of tasks that made life easier, including the creation of hats and basic clothing. The process of rubbing together handfuls of plant fibres to create long threads is perhaps one of the most underappreciated inventions in prehistory. Nowadays we just look at threads like these as office string – but back then making them was a major step for humankind. It led not only to the invention of clothing and blankets but also to the creation of nets, ropes, snares, and fishing lines, to name but a few crucial inventions.

Since then, of course, our range of materials has broadened – bark, cotton, silk, flax, raffia, bird feathers, animal skins, and wool – as have our methods – pounding, curing, weaving, felting, sewing, beading, and dyeing. Among the Ashanti tribe of central Ghana, bark cloth was used for clothing before weaving was introduced. The Ashanti are now highly regarded for their cotton and silk weaving. Intriguingly, Ashanti women may pick cotton or spin materials into thread, but only men are allowed to do the actual weaving. Each of the patterns in their cloth has its own name and each communicates a different message, representing the wearer's social status, clan, or gender.

When there is no need for clothes...

Some tribes in warm climates have no need to invest in extensive wardrobes. Andaman Islanders in the Bay of Bengal, tribes of Papua New Guinea, Australian aboriginal groups, and tribes of tropical America and central Africa are just some of those around the world who wear minimal garments, often making do with a thread, gourd, or looped cloth to protect the genitals. However, even though the warmth of these areas may mean that there is no real need to wrap up, people still tend to "clothe" their bodies with ornaments and body paint.

Adornment in the Amazon

The Kayapo of the Brazilian Amazon wear bright bead bracelets, armlets, anklets, and sashes over their naked bodies, and paint their skin using a mixture of soot and plant extract, such as the juice of the genipap fruit and the urucum seed, which is used throughout the Amazon as a red pigment. The Kayapo believe that their ancestors learned how to live communally from social insects such as bees, which is why mothers and children paint each other's bodies with patterns that look like animal or insect markings, including those of bees. Women also shave a distinctive V-shape into their hair. On ceremonial occasions men wear a flamboyant headdress with outwardly radiating feathers, which represent the universe, and a rope that hangs down the back, symbolizing the cotton rope that the first Kayapo used to descend from the sky.

Opposite: Panara women in the Brazilian rainforest reinforce their group identity by painting themselves identically. Their solidarity has meant that they have survived decades of turmoil, and have managed to return to the land from which they were forcibly relocated in the 1970s.

Top right: A Kayapo woman of the Brazilian Amazon with face paint and the hairstyle of all the women in their tribe. Her hair has grown, but it is still possible to see where a distinctive V-shape was shaved into it.

Bottom right: The juice of the genipap fruit is used to paint a distinctive geometric design on the bodies of Kayapo men.

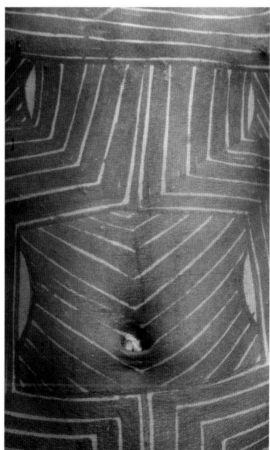

Conveying emotion

Body paint is also used to send out specific signals. In the early years of the 20th century, the anthropologist James Teit studied a Canadian First Nations people called the Thompsons (now more formally known as the Nlaka'pamux) and reported that during ceremonies they painted their bodies with a design that represented their guardian spirit. At other times body paint was used to indicate their emotional state. One widowed woman, recorded by Teit in the 1920s, painted the upper part of her forehead red and the lower part yellow to represent the dawning day. Below each eye were four vertical lines representing tears. The act of painting the body can itself be therapeutic and in this instance it also signalled the woman's special status as a grieving widow.

The Thompsons were not alone in using paint in this way. Aboriginal Australians paint their bodies white when they are in mourning, and in the Xingu area of the Amazon, groups such as the Bororo paint the head and hair red after the death of a relative.

Teit also described Thompson warriors as using paint to advertise their strength and their intentions on their faces. A common design was to paint the face half red and half black. The red was believed to bring luck to the warrior and the black adversity and death to his enemy. Another design featured alternating stripes of red and black that radiated over the chin and jawbone from under the mouth. In this case, the black stripes may indicate how many people the warrior had killed over his lifetime.

Status symbols

The practice of lip enlargement exists in many African tribes: the Lobi of Ghana, the Ubangi of the Congo basin, and the Makonde of Kenya are examples. The general rule is that the women with the largest discs enjoy the highest status (*see also* page 166).

Al Wahibi tribeswomen in the Middle East are veiled to demonstrate their modesty, although their bracelets, anklets, and other jewellery are often clearly displayed, rather like a visible dowry to show a woman's worth within her society. It's perhaps a similar notion to the Western one of regarding the size of a diamond engagement ring as a status symbol.

Taboo and nudity

In Ethiopia, among the Hamar tribe of the Omo Valley, adolescent girls display their bare breasts as a matter of course, as do women of different ages in many other societies around the world. In Western society, however,

Opposite left: Children of the Kayapo tribe are decorated as extensively as adults for ceremonial occasions. This child has a shaved V-shape in his hair, wears strings of beads, and is painted with *karajuru* and genipap juice.

Opposite right: A boy of the Mursi tribe in the lower Omo Valley, Ethiopia, is decorated with a white paste made from clay.

Above left: The ochre-painted face of a boy from the Nuba tribe of Sudan (*see* page 42 and pages 163–5). Bodily decoration is extensive in Nuba culture, where physical beauty is highly prized.

Above right: The face of a man belonging to the Achuar tribe of the Amazon's tributaries in Peru and Ecuador is carefully painted with a design echoing that used in his woven headdress.

a woman strolling down a street bare-chested could face arrest for indecent exposure. Western sensibilities mean that mothers can even feel awkward about breast-feeding a child in public, a fact that probably contributes to the relatively low percentage of breast-fed children in parts of the industralized world.

Clothing, morality, and place are all closely linked. In the industrialized West, a pair of swimming shorts or a bikini is likely to look ridiculous or even obscene when worn away from a beach – such are the confines of occasion, and woe betide any of us who break the rules of our own society without good reason.

Practical clothing

Despite our love of ornament, without practically designed clothing we humans would have never expanded so extensively across the globe. The technology of clothing allowed us to move into areas that had previously been too cold, and thus to gather and hunt for longer periods. Clothing also gave us many other advantages over our natural, naked state. There is an ancient Buddhist saying, "In order to make the whole world comfortable to walk on you would need a lot of leather – but just a little bit of leather will cover your feet and make it possible for you to walk across the whole world." Since the invention of clothes and shoes we have done exactly that – we have walked across the entire planet, precisely because of this technology. Animal skins have been essential wear in cold climates, as can still be seen today in the way the Inuit peoples layer fur and waterproofed skins in order to keep warm and dry, and to avoid frostbite. A naked human would never survive on

One widowed woman painted the upper part of her forehead red and the lower part yellow to represent the dawning day.

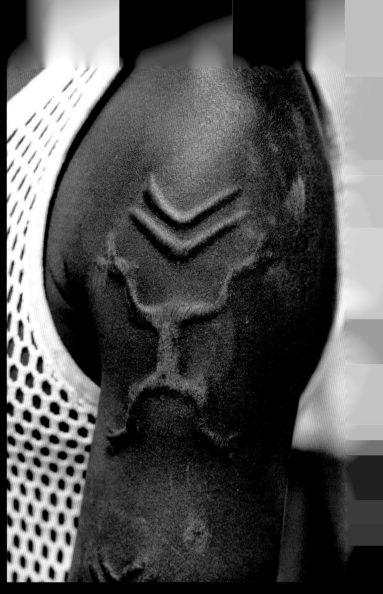

The body beautiful

The Nuba of Sudan wear few clothes and instead use body paint all their lives – even a newborn baby is rubbed with oils and red and yellow ochre. Throughout the various stages of life bodily decoration continues as a celebration of beauty. The designs are there to emphasize the physique, particularly the strength of the young male body. The Nuba have terms for practically all the muscles visible on the surface of the body and also for the depressions between them, including nine words for different parts of the spine.

The young Nuban body must be clean, shaved, and oiled before decoration. During their praise-song dances, the men paint themselves a rich, deep black. They are the centre of attention of the entire group and a man who succeeds in impressing his audience may be rewarded by a girl throwing her legs over his shoulders to indicate that she appreciates his decoration and beauty, and also that she may wish to rendezvous with him later. For the Nuba, nakedness is a way of showing the body at its most beautiful, as a glorious canvas celebrated through paint and careful scarification (see Chapter 7: Belief, Ritual, Healthcare). As men grow older, or if they are injured or incapacitated, they may wear clothing to disguise the fact that they no longer live up to the aesthetic ideal.

Above left: Male members of the Nuba tribe paint their bodies with decorative designs to emphasize their beauty, strength, and physique.

Above right: A Nuban man displays an elaborate scarification.

Right: A Nuban woman with delicate cicatrization scarring. The scars are raised with a fish

the plains and icecaps of the north; if we hadn't developed clothing we would have had to remain creatures of warmer climes.

The parka, a heavy, hooded jacket lined with fur, is now a common part of a Western winter wardrobe, but the original design came from the Inuit of the Arctic, who invented it so that they could survive the frozen north. It was then adapted by the United States military as a practical coat for troops. Among the Inuit the parka may be made with seal or caribou skin and coated with fish oil to keep it waterproof, or it may be a warm fur coat made from fox, polar bear, or wolf. It may also often accommodate a child tucked up inside. The name comes from the Nenets language of the Arctic. An anorak, also a word derived from an Inuit language, is a lighter-weight waterproof garment that can be pulled over the head; the cagoule is a modern version of this.

Footwear – from one extreme to the other

Although clothing can be highly practical, it can also fly in the face of practicality, and nothing shows this contradiction more clearly than the styles of shoe that have developed around the world. Some footwear, such as the snowshoe, ski, and Inuit *mukluk* boot, is resolutely functional and gets the wearer around a freezing environment in the most efficient way possible. Sometimes, in warmer lands, the bare human foot is the best means of navigating terrain, particularly in wet tropical rainforest or across sand that is not too hot. Witness the swift-footed San of the Kalahari Desert in southern Africa, for example, who prefer to walk with bare feet and can recognize each other's footprints. The bare foot can triumph against even the most modern sports shoes, as shown by the Sudanese athlete Amna Bakhit, who won the women's 800-metre event at the Beijing Olympics in 2008 without the benefit of footwear. The "marathon monks" of Mount Hiei in Japan are said to run the equivalent of the length of the equator over seven years, wearing *wajari* – straw sandals – and covering over 80km (50 miles) on a normal day.

The height of discomfort

At the opposite end of the spectrum from shoes designed for comfort and protection is the stiletto heel of the Western world, which reaches ever more vertiginous heights each season. It is designed with an erotic intent, elongating the leg and arching the torso so that the breasts and buttocks protrude.

Even more extreme, and even more erotic in intention, was the lotus shoe of China, designed for a foot that had been permanently disfigured by binding. The lotus foot formed part of the sexuality of the Chinese aristocracy, perhaps because a woman who can hardly walk could be seen as being enticingly passive...

Modesty does not have a constant value across societies – different tribes view it in very different ways – and a Chinese girl who had had her feet bound would think it indecent to let anyone see her artificially compressed toes. Feet-binding, which is thought to have died out in the 20th century, was practised among different ethnic groups in China for over a thousand years. The process began when a girl was five or six years old, and as she grew the bandages were tightened so that the growth of the foot was interrupted. The big toe remained untouched as it is essential for balance, but the forefoot and heel were brought as close together as possible, with the four smaller toes curled under the ball of the foot, creating a soft, fleshy cleft in the arch. This cleft was thought to represent the

> The lotus shoe of China was designed for a foot that had been permanently disfigured by binding.

Above: The bound feet of a woman from China's Yunnan Province. The "lotus" foot shape was achieved by breaking the bones of the four small toes and forcing them under the foot over a period of time. Bound feet were once the ultimate measure of a woman's beauty in some areas of China.

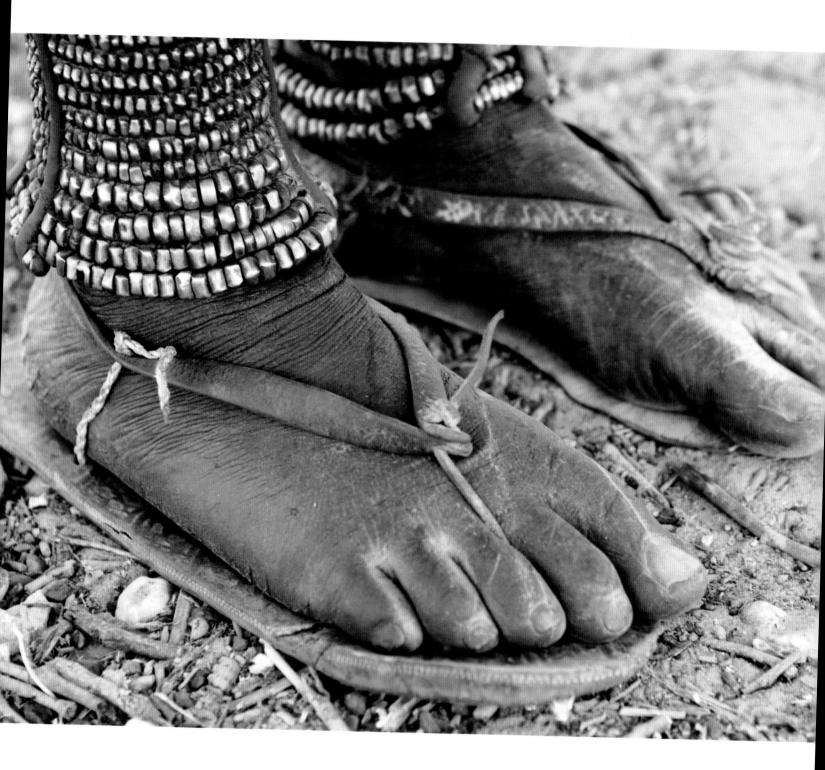

Above: A woman from the Himba tribe of northern Namibia wears beaded anklets to protect her legs from the bites of poisonous animals, and flat shoes suitable for walking long distances.

Dress and Adornment

very essence of a woman's personality. It was regarded as obligatory for aristocrats and very important for prostitutes and concubines, because the foot was used in love-making and thought to be exquisitely erotic. A woman's feet were the exclusive possession of her husband and even close relatives would avoid touching or looking at them in order to preserve her modesty.

Veils and turbans

In some Arabic countries the head must be covered. The Arabic language has around 26 terms for different types of veil, some of which are worn exclusively by men, some by both sexes, and some only by women. In some Arabic societies a woman's veil is sacrosanct and she is not permitted to remove it in front of any man except her husband. Some veils cover the entire body, others only the face or part of the head. In many Arabic countries different veils express the status of the wearer. For the nomadic Bedouin of the deserts, patterns can signify membership of a certain group, and sometimes the same patterns are found on both veils and tents. Among the Rashidi, married women wear a particular mask – the *gina* – consisting of a tube of black cloth that resembles a cone with the top cut off. The tube is slipped over the head so that the woman's shoulders, back, and chest are covered; the opening is then drawn in above the nose and mouth, hiding the bottom half of the face and pulled so tight that the wearer cannot open her mouth wide.

In Cairo before World War I, women appeared in public unveiled as a sign of protest against their lack of status.

In some parts of the world, the veil has been a focus of intense debate. In Cairo before World War I, women appeared in public unveiled as a sign of protest against their lack of status. In Turkey, the *hijab* or headscarf has been banned in civic buildings such as universities since Ataturk's secularization of the Turkish state in the 1920s, though there are calls for this ban to be lifted. In France, a ban on wearing headscarves and other conspicuous religious symbols in schools was imposed in 2004 and in the north of Italy the all-covering *burqa* is not permitted.

A cloth of many colours

Turbans, which are thought to have been a common form of headgear in the Middle East for millennia, since before the spread of Islam, serve the very practical purpose of shielding the wearer from the sun. In medieval Arab communities after the crusades, turbans were used to distinguish people of different religions: Christians wore blue, Jews yellow, Muslims black or white. Turbans can also, in times of conflict or battle, be unwound from the head and used like flags.

Clothing codes

Clothes very quickly became more than just a practical response to the environment. They were – and are – a public symbol that is shared and hopefully understood among the members of the wearer's society. They can attract a marriage partner and good luck, ward off evil influences, and determine status. But any outfit may be open to endless interpretation. A Westerner may wear red and green because she thinks it makes her eyes look attractive, or as a fashion

Clockwise from right: This Iranian woman observes purdah by wearing the *chador* (headdress) and mask. After the revolution of 1979, women who didn't cover their heads could be imprisoned or whipped. Yet in the 2009 uprising, men as well as women wore green veils as a sign of protest against the government; A Tuareg man in Libya with his face and head covered. This is customary for men, but unlike in many other Muslim societies, Tuareg women do not traditionally wear the veil; An Afghan woman wears a full *burqa*, which covers her entire face except for a small region about the eyes, which is covered by a concealing grille; A young Bedouin woman of the Al Wahibi tribe wears a metal face mask. This is traditionally worn at the start of puberty and is considered a sign of maturity; The Sinai Bedouin attach delicate gold and silver beading to veils, making them objects of beauty in themselves.

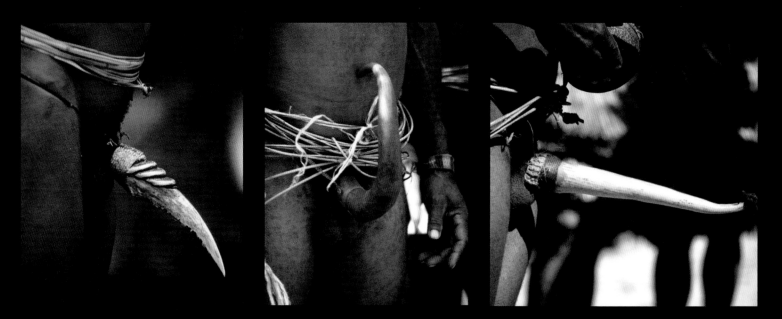

A degree of modesty

Even when the rest of the body is naked, the genitals may be covered for reasons of modesty. Traditionally, the penis may be covered with shells, leaves, nets, or gourds, although in recent times toothpaste tubes, film canisters, and even sardine tins have been used to spare blushes in New Guinea.

Gourds are the hollowed-out shells of hard-bodied fruits, and they are used as water containers, musical instruments, birdhouses, pipes, and even masks. As articles of clothing, they serve as hats in the Philippines and in Africa, and as a covering for the penis in Africa, northern South America, and the south-west Pacific – a fact that came as a shock to a museum curator of the last century who was reported to have blown unsuccessfully into penis gourds, assuming they were a type of trumpet that was particularly difficult to play. In New Guinea, a number of different-sized gourds are worn: in the north they tend to be small and globular, sometimes only the size of a large hen's egg and just covering the tip of the penis; in the central highlands men wear elongated gourds of up to 1m (3ft) long that stick straight upwards – perhaps representing a super-erection. Also in New Guinea, the Umeda hold fertility dances to help the harvest and on these occasions the men wear a large globular gourd over the penis and a belt made of hard seeds round the waist. As they dance the gourd flies upwards in time with their movements and strikes the seeds on the belt, creating a percussive accompaniment to the dance. Sometimes the gourd is filled with stones so that it also acts as a rattle.

Gourds may be left unadorned, engraved with patterns, or decorated with a tassel of fur, or a feather at the tip. They may also be treated with heat and then rubbed with fat so that they have a shiny yellow surface. Men of the Dugum Dani of New Guinea have a complete wardrobe of gourds: some straight, some curved, some globular. The smaller ones will stay on through friction alone, but larger gourds must be attached with a string that ties around the hips or waist. The gourd may also be multipurpose. Some men use them to keep small objects safely and secretly, and others as a holder for a smoking cigar.

Top left: A Kombai man in New Guinea wears a penis sheath made from the beak of a hornbill.

Top centre: The ceremonial costume in Papua New Guinea includes a penis gourd.

Top right: In Sepik, Papua New Guinea, a warrior from one of the highland tribes wears a hollowed-out gourd over his penis.

Above: A Yali man wears a traditional penis sheath while working in fields in the Baliem Valley, West Papua.

Right: Penis gourds are worn in parts of Africa, as shown by this Taneka-Beri man from Benin.

statement, or just be because it is Christmas and she is feeling festive. But how is an outsider to tell the difference?

The message conveyed by clothes is a huge subject and, as with so many areas of human life, it has multiple layers of meaning that are difficult to pin down. But there are some generalities that help us see a larger picture.

Universal colours

There are three colours that seem to be part of a basic language of costume: red, white, and black. Archaeological evidence suggests that they were the first pigments made by humans and the anthropologist Victor Turner believes there is a universal preference for them, as each is a representation of a colour produced by the human body. For the Ndembu of Zambia studied by Turner, white is linked with semen and mother's milk, and therefore reproduction. Red is associated with blood, and hence with war and hunting, and also with the tie between a mother and child. Black represents decay and is associated with death.

Red in tooth and claw

The Tsou tribe of central southern Taiwan is one example of a people who regard the colours of clothes as having huge significance – and, not surprisingly, their clothes are generally red, white, and black. Men wear red as they believe it to be the favourite colour of the god of war.

The Masai of Kenya are known for clothing themselves in beautifully coloured wraps – the women's are called *kanga* and the men's *kikoi* – which usually incorporate some form of red. Culturally, this is an important colour for the Masai: they traditionally created it for their warriors' shields by mixing clay with the red sap of the *Solanum campylae* fruit or even blood taken from their cattle. The Masai's red clothing also stands for power. The men colour their hair red with clay and red ochre, a pigment found in natural form in volcanic regions.

Reading patterns

Design as well as colour can be symbolic: for example, the diamond-shaped patterns on a *panjova*, part of the traditional costume worn by Ukrainian women, are thought to represent the vagina, symbolizing female fertility. The dotted squares around the diamond shapes are likely to be a representation of a sown field – a fertile place. An outsider looking at the pattern would have no idea of the deeper meaning behind it, but for those in the know, its symbolism is clear.

Expressing allegiance

In the industrialized West, we like to think our choice of clothing is exactly that – our choice. We often strive to be unique (but not so weird as to be ostracized) and to express ourselves. We do this via the symbols of our own society. It is our culture that determines and limits what is acceptable in dress and adornment.

In communities that are less concerned with individualism, people are happy to dress similarly, expressing allegiances to certain tribes or groups in the way they dress and clothe themselves. These

Below: Warriors from the Tsou tribe of Taiwan sing to welcome the god of war during the *mayasvi* ceremony. Like many other tribes and cultures, the Tsou associate the colour red with bloodshed and warfare.

allegiances may be permanent (to a tribe) or temporary (to a tribal grouping). In the latter case, the symbolism is much the same as that of a football supporter who wears his team's colours when going to a match – to show he belongs to this particular fan club or social group – but not at other times, when showing this allegiance is less important.

The island of Mindanao in the Philippines is home to 18 different tribal groups. To the outside world, the best known of these is the T'boli tribe, members of which set themselves apart from other groups by their woven clothing, complicated beadwork, and jewellery, often covering their heads with large hats. Clothing is a source of real pride for the T'boli people and is a powerful way for them to differentiate themselves from other tribal groups in the region.

The nomadic Qashqa'i of Iran wear distinctive clothes that distinguish them from non-Qashqa'i people and symbolize their pride in their identity. The women wear long tunics slit up both sides over layers of floor-length skirts. They pay particular attention to their headdresses. A lightweight scarf is worn over the head; its colour is directly linked to a woman's age and status. The colours begin at white when she is a young girl, then move through pale blue, green, and yellow as she passes through stages of early adulthood, to black and brown when she is a mature

woman. A long and often colourful headband (*yayliq*) is wrapped around the head over the scarf, then knotted loosely at the back of the neck so that the ends trail down the woman's back. This way of wearing a headdress is particular to the Qashqa'i. It distinguishes women of different groups from one another and from other tribes in the area who dress in similar ways. The myriad variations also convey subtle messages that only another Qashqa'i woman would understand.

Dressing for equality

In Saudi Arabia, Islam's egalitarian ideal (that everyone is equal in the sight of God) means that many men wear seemingly indistinguishable clothes, although a closer look often reveals subtle differences in the quality of cloth and accessories. However, there are great variations in dress in the kingdom's more remote areas. In the Astir region, the men of the Quatani, a sheep- and goat-herding tribe have adopted a short, wrap-around skirt similar to a kilt as their traditional dress, instead of the more familiar *dish dash* or *thobe* (a long, slim kaftan-like robe).

> Clothing is a source of real pride for the T'boli people and is a powerful way for them to differentiate themselves from other groups in the region.

Sending a message

Across the world people use the way they dress to convey clear messages. For example, in the 1960s, President Kennedy wore his sleeves rolled up, denoting that he was hard-working and not afraid to get his hands dirty; his shirts were often untucked, and his suit had two buttons rather than the traditional three. He even disposed of the traditional top hat for his inauguration speech. His clothes encoded youth and confidence, and his self-assured, carefree style was a radical departure from the grey suit and hat worn by American politicians of the previous decades.

People in different religious groups are often recognized by their clothes. In Jerusalem, for example, Orthodox Jews wear hats and black garments, showing their commitment to their faith. A Cistercian monk is easily seen in a crowd if he is wearing his habit.

Symbolic clothing

The men of the Bakhtiari tribe of Iran attach strong symbolic importance to their appearance – what they wear is determined by their social status. In *The Nomadic Peoples of Iran* (2002), Jean Pierre Digard notes that a leader or rich tribesman who doesn't work with his hands can be identified by his tall, black, cylindrical felt hat (*kola-khosrowi*), wide-legged black trousers (*shawlar-goshad*), which can measure over a metre (yard) round each leg, and a jacket (often Western) over which he wears a blue and white, sleeveless, knee-length woollen *chugha* that hangs over a white cotton belt. As well as indicating the wearer's economic standing in the tribe, and protecting him against the weather, the *kola-khosrowi* can be used to drink from, money can be hidden under it, or it can be waved like a flag to attract someone's attention. A nomad (*lor*), who does a variety of manual jobs, wears a small, felt skullcap and coloured or striped undertrousers that are often rolled up when he is working. His *chugha*, also blue and white, is crossed over and tied firmly around his waist with the belt.

Bakhtiari women are known for their headdresses. They wear a headband decorated with mirror pieces and a brightly coloured veil. The quality of the fabrics a woman chooses, and the cleanliness of her clothing, indicate her status, as does the number of ornaments she wears, such as coins and mirror pieces stitched on to headbands, or pendants displayed on the temples, and their value.

Above: A woman of the Iranian Qashqa'i tribe. The woman wears a traditional long floral-print dress.

Bakhtiari children of both sexes wear jackets, pullovers, and caps studded with amulets that are believed to protect them from misfortune and illness. These come in many forms, such as small bells, pieces of rabbit skin, beads, and animal teeth, which are stitched into the children's garments.

"Readable" clothes

The clothing worn by the Naga tribes of north-east India communicates a precise set of messages as to where in society someone belongs and also demonstrates their status – all this information is as "readable" as if it was written on a badge. Designs and colours may vary not only between tribes but also between clans of the same tribe, and between different villages. Naga men must earn the right to wear certain types of shawl. Different designs, woven patterns, lines, bands, widths, and colours convey different messages. An example is the warrior shawl, *rongsu*. One of the most decorative shawls in Naga culture, it may be worn only by a man who has taken part in the *mithun*-sacrifice feast by providing an animal to be killed in honour of his dead ancestors. This is an extremely significant event that gives Naga men immense social standing.

Among the Yimchunger, a subtribe of the Naga, only a well-respected and experienced warrior is allowed to wear a *rongkhim* shawl. Its pattern, design, and red colour symbolize the shed blood of an enemy. The Yimchunger Naga hold it in such high regard that they believe any man who wears it without being entitled to do so – who is not a warrior – will surely die of disease.

Adornment

Adornment can be rich in symbolism; how we choose to decorate our bodies and draw attention to ourselves tells other people a lot about us. Among the Samburu in Kenya, a headdress made of a lion's mane signifies that a warrior has killed a lion with his spear. It is rather like a military medal: a mark of achievement, and a visual display of bravery and skill. Also in Kenya, a Masai youth who is being initiated into manhood covers his body in red ochre powder mixed with butter to symbolize his fierce and fiery nature. His long, plaited

Opposite top:
In Nairobi, Kenya, a teenage Masai boy is painted with ochre mixed with butter for his initiation into manhood. The vibrant red symbolizes his masculine strength and power as a future Masai warrior.

Opposite centre:
In Venezuela, Yanomano women shave a tonsure in the centre of the heads of their husbands and sons. Over the year this carefully tended bald patch is decorated to show lunar cycles, establishing a visual link between the men of the tribe and tribal mythology.

Opposite bottom:
A Hagen man in Papua New Guinea wears an impressive wig for a sing-sing festival – an occasion of music and dance at which full ceremonial costume is worn.

Together yet apart

In Bhutan, the traditional garments for most Bhutanese are a *goh* for a man and a *kora* for a woman, and are still worn with pride on a daily basis. However, the dress of the Layaps in the Bhutanese Himalayas is different to that of the rest of the country, to distinguish them from other tribes and provide protection against the cold environment. The women wear patchwork skirts woven from yak hair, with dark shawls and conical hats. The men also dress in woven yak-hair garments. This clothing gives them a sense of belonging within their community.

The people of the remote and nomadic Bragpa tribe in the east of Bhutan also emphasize their tribal identity through their dress. Their appearance is fearsome: the men wear animal skins over thick, woven tunics, and distinctive five-pointed felt hats to protect their faces from the region's heavy rains. Even small children have tiny hides covering their clothing. The women wear a red cape over a homespun dress that is normally pulled tight at the waist. These unique garments stand out clearly against the more homogeneous *goh* and *kora* of the kingdom's national dress; the Bragpa cannot be mistaken for any other Bhutanese tribe.

hair is shaved, representing the end of his warriorhood (*see* page 160), and his head is smeared with ochre, after which the ritual that allows him to become a man begins.

The symbolism of hairstyles

The way a person styles their hair can be used symbolically. For example, in preindustrial England, girls wore their hair down as children and pinned it up when they became adults. Among the Bagwa of India, different hairstyles indicate a woman's status as an unmarried girl, married woman, or mother.

In many cultures it is traditional for people to shave their hair when someone dies, as a symbol of mourning and to indicate a new start. In the West, short hair is often a sign of submission, as when recruits have their hair cut on joining the army. And in 1967, Greece's military dictators announced that tourists with long hair were no longer welcome in their country as they associated the style with rebellion.

In the Amazon basin, the Yanomano shave a circle in the centre of their scalps, and the hair around the bald patch is cut in a pudding-basin style, rather like the hairstyle of some European monks. When a child's scalp is shaved for the first time, at about the age of three, he or she is considered to have acquired their individual human soul and therefore their own personality. The shaved area – the tonsure – is carefully tended, and the women of the family cut and shave the heads of their kin.

At feasts and before conflict, the tonsure is painted red with plant dye. Any scars that it shows, particularly if obtained through battle, are a source of great pride as they record an individual's history. The tonsure also represents respect for the moon, which the Yanomano believe is covered with pools of blood – hence the daubing of the scalp with red dye to show lunar cycles.

Wigs for dancing in

In Papua New Guinea, Hagen men wear impressive wigs as a masculine embellishment. They are canopies of clay and hair that completely surround the head and may rest on the shoulders, and are fringed with scarab beetles and marsupial furs, and brightly painted in a variety of patterns. The hair used to make a wig is collected by the owner, usually from other men. Female relatives provide long ringlets for either side. A frame is made with pliant cane sticks bound together with *lianas* (strong, flexible stems of climbing plants) and the hair is sewn on to it. Melted wax is dripped on the hair to set it hard. The wigs are worn for a twirling dance that celebrates pig-killing, mainly to attract women.

Ceremonial and ritual dress

Special costumes are often worn for important ceremonies, events, or stages in life. In the West, the traditional white wedding dress symbolizes the bride's virginal qualities. Similarly, in Japan, the bride often wears a white garment under a colourful wedding kimono – representing a clean start for her new life. A fundamental and common characteristic of humans is a desire to be dressed appropriately for an occasion.

Marriage cloths

The Buna Yoruba of Nigeria have 13 specific, hand-woven cloths that are used in the marriage ceremony. They are placed in the marriage basket that the bride takes to her husband's house, and mark her ritual move. One of the cloths, known

Victorian echoes

A distinctive long dress, reminiscent of the fashions of Victorian England, is worn by Herero women in Botswana and Namibia, and is part of the tribe's heritage. It is thought to have been adopted in homage to Queen Victoria in the late 19th century when Botswana was part of the British Empire. Namibia was then a German protectorate and the dress also shows stylistic links between Herero culture and Germany. Its voluminous skirt sweeps the ground, supported by billowing petticoats, and the dress is bound tightly under the bosom with a belt. It buttons across the left shoulder and under the left arm, and voluptuous sleeves narrow over the forearm to flare again at the wrist. It is customary to combine the dress with a small shawl, and women wearing it are expected to move slowly, with dignity and decorum. The dress can be made of any fabric, and the cloth chosen often proclaims allegiance to specifically Herero concerns. Recently, fashionable fabrics have shown cars, pictures of politicians, printed images of Botswana basketry, maps of Botswana, and outlines of the African continent.

The Herero dress is more commonly worn by older women. Although younger ones wear it on ceremonial occasions, they generally prefer knee-length, Western dresses, which are referred to as *Tswana*-style.

The dress must always be worn with a distinctive headdress made from two scarves smoothed over a horizontal frame. Hat and dress are essential partners: Herero women state they would rather throw their skirt over their heads than be seen wearing the dress without the hat.

as *adofi*, has a black, white, and red striped design and is embroidered with the bride's name. A married woman can wear her *adofi* wrapped around her body as clothing – but only if the marriage ceremony was traditional. For this reason, the cloth has become a symbol of Buna culture.

Adofi mi fe, aso ba mi gb' omo
(Adofi is what I want, the cloth that helps me to carry children)

Buna marriage song

Cloths for occasions

The Ashanti of Ghana wear kente – a ceremonial fabric hand-woven on a horizontal treadle loom – on important social and religious occasions. Strips about 10cm (4in) wide are sewn together and made into larger cloths. Kente has huge cultural significance for the Ashanti, who see it as a visual representation of their history, moral values, philosophy, ethics, political thought, belief systems, and aesthetic principles. The cloths come in varying colours, sizes, and designs and are only worn for significant events.

The women of the Rongmei, a clan within the Naga of north-eastern India, wear skirts specifically designed for ceremonial occasions. These differ in colour, design, and pattern from their everyday skirts. Similarly, the design of the sashes worn by Rongmei men for intertribal dancing ceremonies is more intricate than that of the ones they normally wear.

Opposite left: Like the Suri, the Surma of Ethiopia compete in the donga – a stick-fighting competition in which masculine honour and status are at stake.

Opposite right: Wrestling is popular among tribes of the Xingu, a tributary of the Amazon. At the Kaurup festival in Alto Xingu, men from different tribal groups compete against each other for the respect that comes with strength and fighting skills. Their distinctive red and black body paint indicates which community they represent.

A royal wedding

The wedding of Crown Prince Naruhito of Japan and Masako Owada in 1993 was conducted according to strict Shinto principles. The bride wore a 12-layer kimono, which weighed approximately 13.5kg (30lb), the guests dressed in ancient court attire, and the ceremony re-created a ritual of the ancient Japanese Empire. Photographs of the wedding were broadcast and published throughout the world, and showed no sign that Japan was modern and Westernized – there was not a suit in sight. The country's style magazines emphasized the beauty and timelessness of the ritual, and its wedding industry took advantage of the growing interest in the revival of tradition by renting out imitation 12-layer kimonos.

Costumes for contests

Contests between the men of a tribe, or between tribes, are customary across the world, and involve specific clothing and types of adornment. The Suri of the Ethiopian plains compete in a stick fight, during which they wear colourful headdresses and use chalk paste to paint their bodies with intricate patterns designed to impress the women and intimidate opponents. The fight is a battle of honour and manhood: the man who knocks his opponent down is the winner. The *donga* sticks are 1.8m (6ft) long and are carved with a phallic tip, making an obvious link with sexual potency.

Xingu tribal wrestlers in the remote Brazilian rainforest participate in wrestling and spear-throwing contests as part of a *kaurup* – a festival to honour a chief who has died. The wrestling takes place before and after the funeral, and the contestants use the dark juice of the fruit of the genipap tree to colour their hair red and decorate their bodies with geometric designs.

In Mongolia, wrestlers taking part in a *nadaam*, a traditional festival, wear shirts that cover the arms, neck, and back, but leave the chest and stomach bare. Underpants and high boots are also worn. The costume is designed to deter women from entering the event. It is said that a woman once secretly entered a wrestling competition and won; so, to avoid any future humiliation, the men dress in this unusual way.

Fashion and protest

In parts of the world what people wear has been a battleground in the struggle between colonizers and colonized. In some cases colonial powers imposed their type of clothing on the people they ruled, but in others indigenous groups were able to continue wearing their traditional garments. Today, exotic designs, fabrics, and accessories from around the world are regularly seen on the catwalk, in the high street, and in the wardrobes of the fashion-conscious. The French designer Jean-Paul Gaultier has drawn on styles from sub-Saharan Africa with garments that feature rich beadwork, bodices shaped like African masks, wooden and amber bangles, and intricate feathering.

Clothes with a political purpose

Clothes can be used by indigenous groups to make political statements. Under Mao Zedong, chairman of the Communist Party of the People's Republic of China from 1949 to 1976, the Maoist suit was compulsory clothing and it was dangerous to wear anything that suggested allegiance to an ethnic rather than a state identity. In the 1920s, Ataturk banned the fez as an expression of an old, forgotten Turkey. Ghandi's *dhoti*, which he wore even when he met British royalty, demonstrated his vigorous assertion of a separate Indian identity.

In Nigeria, the Yoruba used indigenous clothing to express their beliefs when nationalism became a strong political movement in the years leading up to the country's independence in 1960. In the early days of colonialism, Western dress had been acceptable and was worn by both men and women, particularly if they had professional jobs.

East meets West

In India in the 1980s, many younger, educated women who wanted to look modern rejected the traditional sari in favour of European-style clothes. However, in the early 1990s it became fashionable in both India and the West, where advertisements promoted the garment for its elegance and sensuality. As well as being embraced by the younger generation of Indian girls, it was worn by women who did not come from Asian backgrounds. The ever-growing popularity of Bollywood has also introduced the sari to a global audience. In addition, the traditional *churidar-kurta* or *salwar kaneez* of south Asia, a full, knee-length shirt worn over loose-fitting trousers, has been adopted by fashionable women on the Asian subcontinent and beyond as being more practical than the sari for everyday wear.

The enduring popularity of these traditional clothes means that women on the subcontinent have no need to wear Western clothes to show that they lead modern and stylish lives.

Some Yoruba mixed European and tribal styles to make a subtle political statement: for example, by wearing indigenous arm and ear jewellery with a dress, Western shoes with traditional loose-fitting *sokoto* trousers, or carrying a handbag while wearing an *iro* – a traditional cloth wrapper.

In Kenya in the 1950s, the Mau Mau rebellion against British rule, which originated with the Kikuyu tribe, called for the systematic rejection of European clothing. This was in support of Eliud Mathu, the first African in the Kenyan legislative council, who had torn off his Western jacket during a public meeting, crying: "Take back your civilization – and give me back my land."

In Algeria, also in the 1950s, the enforced unveiling of women under French rule was a metaphor for the rape of Algerian society. The veil became a symbol of resistance, and was worn defiantly by women who supported the country's independence. In South Korea, many progressive female members of the legislature wear Western clothes, whereas those who are more traditional wear the *hanbok*: a blouse-shirt and a full wrap-around skirt, usually in bright colours. In both cases clothes are a visual demonstration of political allegiance.

Going undercover

Effective solutions to evading detection when hunting are found in the simplest tribal clothing designs. Rather than wear the fatigues favoured by the military in the industralized world, tribes have developed their own ways to go undercover. Throughout Australia, aboriginal tribespeople cover their bodies with red ochre, earth, or clay, depending on the terrain. Kangaroo hunters use blue soil for mud flats and ochre for laterite zones. In the Kalahari in southern Africa, the San paint red and yellow stripes on their bodies in imitation of the colours of the land. To stalk ostrich, they carry the bird's head on a long, pliant stick and conceal their bodies while they sneak up on their prey. Likewise, in North America, a tribesman hunting bison wore a wolf skin and moved like a wolf; this allowed him to approach the herd without alarming the animals, as bison did not fear a solitary wolf.

Kangaroo hunters use blue soil for mud flats and ochre for laterite zones.

Opposite top:
A Bragpa man wears an animal-skin hat to combat the low temperatures of high-altitude Bhutan.

Opposite bottom left:
Victor Piak, a Nenet reindeer herder, wears traditional reindeer-skin clothing in western Siberia, Russia.

Opposite right:
Mongolian parents and their daughter wear traditional *del* coats in front of their *ger* in the Gobi Desert.

Functionality

Across the world, tribal peoples have developed clothing that enables them to function with optimum effectiveness in the environments in which they live, and survive in extreme temperatures.

In the Mongolian region, where men of the Darhad tribe herd animals on horseback rather than with dogs and need to ride at great speed standing upright in their stirrups, both men and women wear *del* coats. These are long, loose gowns that are cut from a single piece of fabric, wrapped around the body, and girdled with a sash. They are comfortable on horseback and are worn over trousers, which protect the rider's legs from chafing and temperatures that are below freezing for nearly half the year. Both the *del* and trousers are folded rather than hung for storage – an important criterion for nomadic tribes.

The Bedouin of the Arabian peninsula wear a long, loose robe that keeps them as cool as possible in the baking desert. In particular, their headgear, a cloth worn over the head and secured with a rope, is a true multitask garment: for example, it can be rapidly adjusted to cover the face in a sandstorm.

The Nenet reindeer herders of the Yamal peninsula in Siberia, where temperatures can plummet to –30°C (–22°F), wear a *malista*, a combination of boots and hooded outer tunic. The boots are made from two layers of fur placed back to back so that the fur is both on the inside and outside. Like a fisherman's waders, the boots are tied over the legs and around the waist. Fur layered around the cuffs and hood of the tunic keep body heat in for ultimate warmth on the tundra. Even today, this type of garment is much more effective than a jacket made from man-made fibre.

Whether designed for survival or beauty, tribes dress their bodies with resourceful inventiveness to create a truly global catwalk of clothing and style.

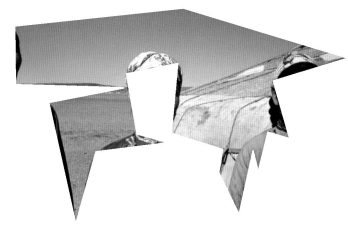

3 House, Shelter, Home

In its most basic sense, housing means shelter or a way of providing shelter, but of course a home is much more than this. A home is as essential to human survival as food and water, but it doesn't only protect us from the elements. Le Corbusier's famous epigram that a house is a "machine for living" describes the home as the place where we go about the business of life. It is where we care for most of our bodily needs, where we store our possessions, where we conceive and rear our children.

So what makes a house a home?

We create a home both to seek privacy and in order to fulfil the basic domestic, social, and personal aspects of family life. Physical and mental health, working efficiency, emotional security, and social status are all likely to be influenced by housing conditions. For most people, home is their base, their space, the place where they feel grounded and "at home" – far from the mayhem of the outside world. It is the same all over the world, whether "home" is a flat in London, Sydney, or New York, a Fulani homestead in West Africa, or a Mongolian *ger*.

Home is not just a fixed place; it can also be a state of mind. We can "feel at home" in a hotel room after just a few days, while many people continue to refer to their parents' house as "home" long after they have moved into their own place.

A home can be anywhere – the place where we grew up, our tribal ancestral lands, the house we live in with loved ones, or the place we rest our heads. It changes over time and experience. As David Steindl-Rast, the 20th-century philosopher and monk, once said, "Home is where we start from, but home is also where we are bound for, the place we always seek."

No fixed abode

Perhaps the starkest reminder of what home means can be drawn from its absence. Walk through an urban area late at night in any industrialized country and you will see "homeless" people on the streets. They are classed legally as having "no fixed abode" and are often marginalized in society. Completely different are those who choose to be of no fixed abode, preferring to travel around the world, seeking adventure. And of course, being of no fixed abode is a fundamental way of life for many tribes, such as the Penan of Borneo or the nomads of Saharan Mauritania. It is this very fact – that groups have no ties to a specific place or space – that allows them to move freely with their herds, following the seasons, the sands, or the new pastures.

Simple shelters

In his 1876 book *The Habitations of Man in All Ages*, the French architectural theoretician and historian Eugène-Emmanuel Viollet-le-Duc (1814–79) tried to show how shelter-making began. Among other designs, he illustrated structures made of tree branches tied together at the top, with "walls" built up by weaving more flexible twigs and branches through the main framework. This is the basic concept of a Native American wigwam or, if covered with skins, a tepee.

Previous page:
An Akha family on
the balcony of their
house in Ban Nam Sa
Akha village high on
a mountain slope in
Laos. An Akha house
is built by the entire
village, and once
it is ready a small
pig is ceremonially
killed. The folds on
the pig's liver are
read to discern
the fortune of the
house's inhabitants.

Opposite: A view
over the rooftops of
a Dogon village near
Bandiagara, Mali.

Right: Two Dassanech
children relax outside
their family home in
Ethiopia's Omo
Delta. The dome-
shaped construction
is covered with hides
and mats made from
the papyrus that
grows in the delta.

A tepee has a frame of long poles tied together at the top. Its outer walls are traditionally skins arranged to allow for a flap doorway and a top flap that can be adjusted to control air circulation and to let daylight in and smoke out. The entire structure is easy to take down, pack up, and transport when it is time for the owner to move on to a new hunting ground.

This simple shape has been adopted by tribal communities all over the world, using materials available locally. Among the Nyangatom of Ethiopia, for example, the outer layer consists of grasses and sticks rather than skins. Modern tepees are also sold in the industrialized world to people who may well have houses of their own, as an ideal way of getting back to nature.

The needs of nomads

For many tribes, nature and its seasons determine where they will set up home. In Mongolia, the Darhad year revolves around finding pasture for herds, which may mean that a family moves six times in 12 months – food for thought in the industrialized world, where moving house is regarded as a stressful event on a par with divorce or the death of a loved one. In autumn, Darhad families move east over the high Khoridal Saridag mountains, returning after a long winter during which conditions can be particularly tough.

In an extreme climate, where temperatures fall as low as –50°C (–58°F), home is a matter of life and death. Sudden blizzards mean that the Darhad must be able to erect their shelters quickly and efficiently when they decide they need to rest. Their answer to this problem is a circular tent called a *ger*, based on a vertical frame of lattice strips that can be put up and taken down easily. Once up, the frame is cleverly expanded and securely tied into a dome shape. This gives maximum internal space with minimum external surface area, thus reducing heat loss and saving covering material. For added protection against the elements, the *ger* is always positioned so that the door faces south, sheltered from the cold north winds.

> In Mongolia, the Darhad year revolves around finding pasture for herds, which may mean that a family moves six times in 12 months.

The roof is often made of willow strips and two semicircular quilts, each cut in the middle to fit around the "roof wheel". Further insulation is provided by four felt or quilt wall coverings, attached to the outside of the trellis walls, and an outer cotton cover enclosing the whole. One of the ties of the roof-wheel covering acts as a shutter cord, which opens to reveal a smoke hole and a window; the Darhad have a traditional method of telling the time by the position of the sunlight through the opening in the roof. In summer, the quilt band at the foot of the wall, sometimes replaced with wooden slats, can be raised to allow air to circulate inside.

Different homes for different seasons

The Tuareg of the Sahara use a variety of dwellings. Agriculturalists who have become more sedentary may live in square or beehive-shaped huts, or even semisubterranean ones. On the other hand, those who remain nomadic believe that they will become ill if they stay in a house for too long. The long, dry spells of the Saharan climate mean that skin tents, which absorb heat, are impractical for year-round use; nonetheless they are the preferred dwellings of the Tuareg

Opposite bottom left: An Uzbek *ger* near Maydena, Afghanistan. The *ger*, a traditional nomadic tent made of felt, has been the abode of the nomads of central Asia from ancient times to the modern day.

Opposite bottom right: Kazakh *ger*, Akkol Canyon, Kazakhstan. The *ger* has many qualities: it is portable yet robust; quick to erect and dismantle yet stable and secure; and warm in the bitter winters yet cool in the baking summers.

Even nomads have status symbols

Among the nomadic Bakhtiari of Iran, one look at a particular camp will tell you the season in which it was pitched in. Tents erected in summer are light and open; in winter they are a lot bigger and better insulated. The traditional material is goat hair, woven into strips that are then sewn together to make a black canopy. The quality of the tent says a lot about the economic status of its owner: large tents made of more than 10 poles in good condition are associated with the wealthy, while tents in poor condition, with visible patches, belong to those with less money. Social status can also be noted from the size of an encampment: over 10 tents signify a chief's residence; five or fewer indicate transient nomads.

Left: In the Zagros Mountains of Iran, Bakhtiari herders camp on pastures during the summer months. The tribe remains nomadic, but is becoming increasingly sedentary. Here a Bakhtiari woman is making *dour* (yoghurt) in a churn made of goat-skin leather.

nomads, who switch to them as soon as the cooling rains begin. These tents are made by tanning skins, usually those of Barbary sheep, and then treating the leather with butter and red ochre, which makes the tent waterproof and gives it a vermilion hue.

Elsewhere in the world, Berbers in the deserts of Morocco use tents made from woven strips of black goat-hair or camel-hair wool. The Fulani, West African nomadic pastoralists, use simple shelters built with saplings planted in a circle and bent over to make a frame that is then covered with woven mats. When the group moves on, they take the mats with them but leave the saplings planted in the ground, where they may serve as a base for future dwellings.

The Gurani, Kurdish nomads of Azerbaijan, settle in village houses during the long, cold winter months, but in summer they travel across the mountain pastures of the Turkish–Iranian border, living in lightweight tents whose walls are made of canes individually wrapped with coloured wools. The wrapped canes are bound together on a loom to make a screen with a large-scale pattern. The Gurani's easy mobility between summer and winter residences is fundamental for a life that follows the seasons.

Moving is also a way of life for many of the rainforest tribes of the Amazon and South-East Asia. The Penan of Borneo are able to leave their *selap* (huts) quickly and set up camp in another part of the forest. They have very few possessions: everything they own can be carried with them in backpacks made from rattan. The *selap* themselves are built about 1.2m (4ft) off the ground, using thick poles tied together with the ever-useful rattan strips. They are roofed with giant palm leaves or, increasingly, plastic tarpaulins – the Penan recognize a serviceable material when they see one. Above a hearth of dried mud are wooden racks used for drying firewood and for storing cooking equipment and other items that need to be kept dry. Each Penan family usually builds one hut for general activities and another, smaller one for sleeping in.

A portable living space

The reindeer-herding Lapps of northern Scandinavia, who now mostly live in timber cabins, have a traditional tent that was the portable home of previous nomadic generations. The simplest sort was made by bending two branches of birch to make an umbrella-shaped frame that was then covered with skin. The hearth was in the centre of the tent and at the back was a small shrine with its own door, where the headman kept a divination drum to use in prayer.

In Siberia, Nenet reindeer herders are also nomadic. During migrations they move as often as every other day. Each family has its own portable living space, called a *chum*, which is made of reindeer skins laid over a skeleton of long wooden poles. Many of the poles have special positions and orders in the structure and are not interchangeable. The choice of *chum* site is based on pasture, relief, and ground quality, and of course having a water source nearby is important wherever you are in the world. When the head of the herding group or brigade decides on a site, he pushes his reindeer-driving stick into the ground to show where he wants the centre of the *chum* to be. The area may have many *chums* set up in it, all belonging to

The choice of *chum* site is based on pasture, relief, and ground quality, and of course having a water source nearby is important wherever you are in the world.

Opposite: A Lapp craftsman sits on a bed of birch branches and reindeer hides as he cooks coffee on the fire in his hut. Huts are made of forest wood and grass.

Below: Lapps use small, elevated buildings for the dry storage of goods while they are herding their reindeer on the tundra.

different families within a brigade. From the moment the head pushes in his stick, this small section of an inhospitable land starts to become a home.

Inducements to settle down?

Strangely, nomadic people seem to face continual pressure to abandon their way of life. In Europe, the powers that be constantly pressurize Romany communities to stay at a fixed address. Similarly, the Chinese authorities have tried to keep nomads in Tibet under closer control by insisting that their traditional yak-hair tents be traded for undecorated cotton tents provided by the state. The government claimed that these tents would be healthier, though in fact they offer less protection from wind and rain. Many nomads continue to use the yak-hair tent, decorated with appliqué motifs of Buddhist prayer wheels, which serve both as a sign of worship and as a signal of defiance to the government.

Missionaries in Africa and South America have often arrived among nomadic communities and built schools and houses. This encourages, and in some cases coerces, tribes to abandon their nomadic way of life, as healthcare and education are provided only if they settle in one place. Since the 1970s, along the Rio Javari, a remote western tributary of the Amazon, the Matses – "the people of the jaguar" – have settled into village life for the first time, because of the presence of a Catholic mission and a clinic. In its early days the village was pretty enough, with a longhouse surrounded by smaller family dwellings, but it stank terribly of sewage – a problem the Matses had never encountered before.

> The Chinese authorities have tried to keep nomads in Tibet under closer control by insisting that their traditional yak-hair tents be traded for undecorated cotton tents provided by the state.

Vernacular Architecture

No-one can say how many dwellings there are in the world, not even to the nearest hundred million. It is possible that there are a billion dwellings to house the world's population of over six billion people. Of these, only a minuscule proportion will have been designed by professional architects. The rest are designed by the people who live in them, and frequently built by them too. This is what is meant by "vernacular architecture": buildings designed by people using local materials to make their homes.

Vernacular architecture includes timber-framed English inns, Swazi thatch "beehive" huts, and the thin-walled mud domes of Cameroon. In the Western world, it has echoes of history and makes popular homes or holiday retreats for those seeking a connection with a romanticized past; living in a crofter's cottage on a Scottish mountain gives an everyday reminder of the Gaelic highland tradition, and in North America a log cabin reflects life on a forgotten frontier. In the West, we like to preserve these links with our heritage and, despite the onslaught of the development juggernaut, the same applies to the vernacular architecture of other parts of the world.

The notion of the "primitive hut" is a commonly used, hazy stereotype that neglects the complexity, functionality, and beauty of many vernacular designs. In the developing world, there is often pressure to abandon traditional homes for modern housing built in the Western style. But such housing schemes often cater only for the barest necessities of an industrial workforce. Does the accommodation of the township of Soweto really provide a better quality of life than the beautiful and practical traditional homes of South Africa?

Opposite top left:
A nomadic camp of felt *ger* in the Terkhin Valley, Mongolia.

Opposite bottom left:
Baka pygmies in Central Africa live in huts called *mongulu*. These are typically dome-shaped structures made of bowed branches and covered in large leaves

Opposite centre:
Beehive-shaped houses of dried clay in the Ghab Valley, Syria.

Opposite top right:
A subterranean Berber home in Matmata, Tunisia. It consists of a courtyard dug into soft sandstone, into which a labyrinth of small rooms for sleeping, grain storage, and

family gatherings is cut. The rooms are connected by narrow passageways.

Opposite bottom right: An Inuit stands on a snow block to build the highest layer of an igloo in north-west Greenland.

Tribal style

Some tribes in Polynesia, the islands of the central Pacific, have a role for master craftsmen, but they are the exception: most people build their homes with their own hands. Tribal houses are often circular, a design that can be traced straight back to nature. The natural world is rarely square; shelters built by birds, insects, and other wild creatures are more often than not rounded in form. A circle is also the geometric figure that will enclose the largest area within the smallest perimeter – an important quality if you are short of space or competing with other groups for resources. Plus, it uses the smallest amount of building material.

In South Africa, Zulu cosmology is permeated by the notion of the circle and, at the height of Zulu power in the 19th century, *kraals* (villages) could be almost 2km (over a mile) in diameter with more than a thousand circular huts. Cattle were kept inside the circle in order to protect them from thieves. Today, the area covered by a Zulu village is smaller, but the dwellings are domed masterpieces of woven grass. Among the Zulus' neighbours, the Swazi, building the frame of the hut is man's work; it is then covered by mats woven by the women from several types of grass. These provide superb insulation against the changing temperatures, which in Swaziland vary regularly from 35°C (95°F) to −4°C (25°F).

A home in the ice and snow

A circular structure was also used by the peoples of the Arctic in the creation of igloos. The Inuit of Greenland and Alaska rarely built snow houses, but they were common among the Central Inuit and regularly used by Netsilik groups in northern Canada as late as the 1960s.

Right: A Karo village in the Omo Valley of Southern Ethiopia. The Karo are pastoralists who live among their livestock. Here, the twig fenced cattle enclosures can be seen between the houses.

Before building began, the snow's consistency was tested using a caribou antler as a probe, as the best blocks were those made of snow from a single fall. Once the area had been chosen, it was cleared of loose snow and blocks were cut using a slightly curved ivory snow knife. Next, a circle was inscribed in the snow and the blocks laid in a ring and placed so that they leaned inwards, forming the first layer of a continuous spiral. One man worked inside the dome and another outside it to stack the blocks; any gaps were filled with loose snow. Once the dome was complete, an opening was made near the floor level and a tunnel built for the entrance. This could be set lower than the internal floor level, so that cold air remained trapped there and did not enter the igloo. Some tunnels were even dug underground. Inside the igloo the tunnel was closed with either a snow-block door or a bear-skin curtain.

Inside the dome were two levels: a platform for living and sleeping and at floor level a general-purpose area for cooking and repairing tools. Some Inuit groups lined the roofs with caribou hides, cleverly leaving a small air-space for additional insulation and to prevent the heat melting

the snow walls. A combination of blubber lamps and body heat made it possible for the temperature inside an igloo to reach 15.5°C (60°F), when outside it might be –40°C (–40°F). To let in light, a window was created by making an arched opening over the entrance. In place of glass was either a translucent layer of sewn seal intestines or a block of clear ice made by melting snow in a seal-skin bag and using the resulting curved shape to fit the surface of the dome.

Nowadays, an Inuit igloo is normally used only as a temporary shelter, for example during a hunting trip, as the dome shape is very resistant to the strong Arctic winter winds. This shape is exactly what a computer-aided design package will come up with if given those environmental constraints – the virtual wind tunnel will always produce an igloo.

More than just a dwelling

In its simplest form, a house is a structure built for people to live in. But the word is also used in a much broader sense – for a building that is the centre of activity of an organization, a family, a tribal group, or a couple. In the

West, two people choosing to live together are taking a significant step, because setting up house with someone is an important symbol of commitment.

A place of worship, a sign of prestige

A tribal house serves many functions. It can be seen as an item of material culture, an object with symbolic meaning, or the focus of domestic activities. The Mongolians consider their *ger* a model of the universe in miniature, with the roof as the sky, the window as the sun, and the hearth as the sacred centre. Among the Kachin people of Myanmar and China, the house is pivotal to thinking about politics, economics, and religion. Vocabulary and grammar reflect these basic beliefs. The Kachin organize themselves into tribal, clan, and household groups. Members of a clan do not necessarily live together, but their social group is referred to as "people under one roof"; a family is *nta masha* or "people of the house". The house is also a religious building – a place to perform rituals. Inside a chief's house there is usually an elaborate shrine to the chief sky spirit, Madai. Each household has a shrine to the spirits of the ancestors, but the right to sacrifice to Madai rests with the chief.

A Kachin household is created through marriage, a time when a man is said to "extend the roof" of his house and, with his wife, become its joint owner. The architecture of the house is equally important. There are clear design differences between the chief's house and the homes of those of a lower social

Opposite: An Inuit uses a snow knife to build an igloo with large blocks of snow in north-west Greenland.

Above: The interior of a traditional Inuit igloo in Manitoba, Canada.

status. A chief's is always much bigger – an obvious sign of prestige – but it also has oversized hardwood posts, which indicate chiefly rank.

Likewise, in the Mongolian *ger*, decoration has traditionally corresponded with rank: historically, only nobles were allowed painted and carved posts. With the spread of socialism in the Mongolian People's Republic, these decorative features have become common as the distinction between nobles and those of less lofty birth has been blurred.

Part of a ritual

The Gabra live in one of the most inhospitable regions of the world, the Chalbi Desert, which straddles the border between Kenya and Ethiopia. They are nomadic camel herders for whom a house has enormous symbolic and ritual meaning. A Gabra marriage actually focuses on ritual house building.

Preparations for a wedding begin up to three months before the event. Building a house is regarded as women's work and the female members of both families spend the weeks leading up to the celebration scouring the desert for scarce materials that can be skilfully made into household items such as gourds, door arches, mats, and bowls.

The groom goes into the desert in search of acacia branches to make the circular base for his marital tent, which will be built near his father's house, but this is the only input he will have into his new home. Meanwhile, the bride's mother's tent is carefully disassembled, certain parts of it being kept aside to be used for her daughter's residence. As with any tribe whose lifestyle depends upon efficient movement, the Gabra women's ability to take down a tiny tent, frame by frame, mat by mat, and then rapidly load their lives on to a camel caravan is impressive.

> As with any tribe whose lifestyle depends upon efficient movement, the Gabra women's ability to take down a tiny tent, frame by frame, mat by mat, and then rapidly load their lives on to a camel caravan is impressive.

The bride's family travels on camelback across the desert, often trekking for days to the groom's village, where they carefully unload their belongings and build the much-anticipated bridal tent. The various rituals carried out at this stage include the groom's father chanting and blessing the new tent with milk, coffee, and butter (all valuable commodities). Once the tent has been assembled, the groom performs a ceremony to mark the all-important first fire in his new home.

Back at the bride's camp, the carefully guarded young girl helps to rebuild what is left of her mother's tent – much of it has been used in making the bridal tent, so the women deftly reconstruct a liveable space out of virtually nothing. Older Gabra women, widows especially, are recognized by their tiny tents, which are often just big enough to lie down in.

On the final day, the bride arrives at her new home in an amazing camelback enclosure. Every inch of material on the camel's back is stunning – the saddles, the beads, the decorations. The bride and groom then carry out marriage negotiations and as the day draws to a close they are finally left to consummate their marriage by sleeping next to each other in their new home.

The household

In most societies across the world, the smallest important social group is the household, which usually consists of people who are relatives but may or may not live under one roof. Many communities have living arrangements whereby men, women, and youngsters of the same family live in different huts or places.

Tune in, drop out

Domes are also the usual default shape chosen by Westerners who opt out of the mainstream and build their own homes. During the hippy era, self-built communes sprang up in America and Europe, one of the most famous being Drop City in southern Colorado. In 1965, three people decided to buy 2.3 hectares (6 acres) of goat pasture and see what happened. A community sprang up, consisting mostly of people in their twenties, who created a series of domes based on a model that a local farmer happened to have in his yard. The result resembled a large sculpture, but was also the community's home. The domes could be single-standing to house a family, or merged to create large complexes for bigger gatherings.

Each of the planes of the domes needed to be covered and this was done with whatever could be found – lumber, railway sleepers, insulation sheeting, plastic bags. Homes emerged from what had been thrown away as rubbish, a fitting vernacular architecture for the modern age. Drop City was abandoned by 1977, but remnants of this experiment in vernacular building remain at the site today.

Above and below: Drop City's first dome, built in June 1966, was made by piecing together sections of car metal. Based on a zonohedron (an "exploded" rhombic dodecahedron), its parallel zones were stretched apart to create a spacious interior. It proved to be the building block of one of the most famous communes of the 1960s and 1970s, and eventually contained a community kitchen, an entertainment space, a film workshop, bathrooms, and a visitors' area.

For example, the Fulani nomads of the Sahel region in West Africa are Muslims and the men are permitted to have up to four wives. A Fulani homestead, the area where the household lives, is divided into two parts, with the wives living in two shelters in one half, and the men, boys, and cattle spending their time, both waking and sleeping, in the other.

The Dogon live on the Bandiagara escarpment of Mali, West Africa. They view "home" not simply as a building, but as a series of stages, which can be represented by several buildings. When a woman marries, she lives with her father during the day but sleeps with her husband at night. This continues until she has had at least three children, which gives her the status to leave her father and set up a separate home with her husband. For the Dogon, a person's home is related to their individual development.

The design of a Dogon home is based on the body, and different parts of the house symbolize male and female body parts to represent the man and woman who will create and raise children in the home. The grand entrance of the house symbolizes the labia of the vagina, the entrance into the maternal womb. The main area is windowless and dark inside, and represents the inside of a woman's body. The ceiling represents the man: his skeleton is shown by the beams of the roof; the four supporting posts are the couple's arms.

Sex and separation

The Dogon house, with its allusions to the female body, shows a correlation between architecture and gender, which is also reflected in the widespread tribal custom of

The multipurpose longhouse

The Iban of the Sarawak region of Borneo live together as communities in longhouses that sit on stilts facing the banks of waterways. Raised on massive ironwood pillars and built of ironwood planks, they are immensely durable. A single longhouse may be as long as 300m (1000ft) and usually accommodates the entire village, as many as 500 people. Structurally, it consists of a series of family units arranged side by side. The same term, *bilik*, refers both to the unit itself and to the family group that occupies it. Membership of a *bilik* may be acquired by either birth or marriage and the *bilik* family is often made up of at least three generations: grandparents, sons and daughters, their spouses, and their children.

Each *bilik* normally has its own solid door, an equal-width section of the common area on to which all rooms open, and an equal-width section of the porch, which is made of split bamboo laid across supporting logs. The *bilik* is a family living-room, used for sleeping and a variety of domestic tasks, as well as for storing heirlooms. It is separated from other *bilik* by wooden walls. On one side of these walls, the *bilik* units represent each family's domestic space, symbolizing its existence as a household group, while the open gallery on the other side is a public space, symbolizing the longhouse as a whole, collective group of people. The kitchen area is sometimes found within the *bilik*, but may be a separate room added on to the back, or in a building a short distance away, reducing the risk of fire and smoke damage to the longhouse.

The main corridor of the longhouse is divided into three parts. The space in front of the *bilik* door belongs to each family unit, but the rest of the corridor is public space and is used to walk around the longhouse. Opposite the family space is the *ruai*, a workspace that runs down the middle of the gallery, where looms are set up for cloth, and nets and rattan baskets are made. The *pantai*, the space where guests can sleep, is along the outer wall. Under the middle of the longhouse roof is a space known as the *sadau*, where food is stored. As is common in other parts of Indonesia, pigs and chickens live underneath the house between its stilts.

The Iban are not as nomadic as the Darhad of Mongolia or the Nenet of Siberia. However, they do practise shift cultivation and every 15 or 20 years they generally move to more fertile areas, when the land they have been working on is exhausted. They may also move because their longhouse has been burned down by hostile tribes.

Opposite top left: An Iban longhouse situated beside a river in Sarawak, Borneo.

Opposite bottom left: The main corridor of the longhouse, showing the *ruai*, the workspace for weaving and basketry.

Opposite right: Iban women sieve rice on the communal terrace of a longhouse in Sarawak, Borneo.

separating houses into male and female areas. This influences the design and decoration of the home and affects how the space is used. In the Melanesian islands of the western Pacific, the very posts of a house are carved to represent men and women: the outer ones are sculpted in the shape of men, and are positioned around central posts, which are designed as female figures. Women usually stay within the area that these posts define, and are excluded from certain activities in the male zone.

Different parts of the house symbolize male and female body parts to represent the man and woman who will create and raise children in the home.

Gender distinctions affect all aspects of the Rindi house in Sumba, Indonesia. From the very beginning, even during its construction, the building is divided into male and female areas. The erection of four main posts – the two on the right side of the house are classified as male and those on the left as female – must be performed in a specific order. The first post to be erected defines an area at the front of the building, on the right side; it is associated with religious service, and is a place where offerings are made, and ancestors and spiritual beings are addressed. The second post is also placed to the right side, towards the back of the house, and indicates the area where men kill animals for sacrifice. The third post to be put up is positioned on the left of the house, towards the back, in the part of the house used mainly by women in their female tasks of caring for pigs and chickens. Also on the left side of the house, towards the front, the fourth post marks an area where women prepare and serve rice. The main platform in the house is symbolically divided into a left-hand female side and right-hand male side.

The Acehnese of Sumatra also associate male and female with different areas of the house, but their spatial oppositions are different to those of the Sumbanese. Rather than correlating the men's area with the right-hand side of the building, and the women's with the left, the contrast between male and female is reflected in the front and back parts of the house. The front is for the men. It is public and is used for formal occasions; it is also where the male veranda is situated. The female-associated back of the house is a less-organized, informal place that includes the veranda used by the women. It is a private, everyday area, which also serves as a vegetable garden and rubbish dump. Not far from here is the kitchen, where much of the women's work is done. The most sacred area is a platform high in the roof where ancestral heirlooms and valuables are stored. The lowest point of the house, underneath the main housing structure, is a space where rice and weaving looms are stored and poultry is kept in pens.

Two main pillars are erected during the construction of an Acehnese house. The first is thought of as being male and is known as the "king" pillar (much as, in the industrialized world, a linchpin is also known as a kingpin) or "auspicious" pillar. It is situated towards the centre of the house, on the right side of the shelf where offerings are made to ancestors. The second pillar, the "lady" or "queen" pillar, is opposite to the auspicious pillar. Both are lavishly decorated during

their erection: the king pillar with one of the male householder's shirts, and the queen pillar with a blouse belonging to his wife. Offerings are made and the ritual of "tying of the soul" of the two pillars is performed. This symbolizes the sexual union of the man and woman. The main bedroom is the innermost room in the house, and is positioned between the pillars.

The longhouses of the Barasana of Colombia have a front door used by men and a back door for women. The rear part of the house is screened off to form the female area where women prepare cassava and tend to the children. The men work at the front of the house, making baskets; at night they smoke tobacco and chew coca in the central area. This space is used for meals during the daytime, and also for ritual dances when the participants weave, single file, around the building's eight major upright posts. The men and women use different paths between the house and the river: the men make their way through the front door past a clearing, *maka*, from which they can take paths through the rainforest (where they hunt) to the river. The women leave by the back door and follow a separate path to an area of agricultural land, known as the *chagra* (where they practise slash and burn farming) and then to the river.

In Siberia, Nenet *chum* sites are also split into male and female spaces. The men work behind the *chum* and the women carry out their daily tasks in front of the tents.

Men only

The Kwoma tribe of Papua New Guinea has ceremonial houses where male members of the community meet to interact and perform rituals. These are generally located in the centre of the village and are easily distinguishable from the homes in which the men live with their wives and children. The houses are made of timbers, which are elaborately carved and painted with illustrations of Kwoma cultural heroes and masculine stories and myths. In the lead-up to male initiation rites, the young men may stay in the houses for several months preparing themselves for their transition into manhood.

Along the Sepik River in New Guinea, the Abelam tribe build men's ceremonial houses known as *haus tambaran*, where male-only initiation rites and rituals that emphasize male dominance and prestige are performed. These have triangular facades as high as 19.8m (65ft) that are raked forward so that they loom over people standing or walking below them. They are decorated with vigorous paintings of clan spirits, who are represented inside the house by huge carved figures kept in the inner sanctum. These are displayed to men only at the final stage of their initiation into adulthood, which occurs at the end of a lengthy ceremonial cycle that can take up to 30 years. The emphasis on repeated male-only rituals among the Abelam is thought to confirm group identity between men, and means

The head of a household is allocated a space in the centre of his *chum*, behind the table. However, Nenet women, whose activities are concerned with heating and cooking, sleep and work closer to the entrance of the *chum*, near the stove. They are forbidden to cross an imaginary line that runs through the tent from front to back of the tent.

A woman's work...

The division of space within a house is widely used to distinguish between male and female tasks, but among the Dassanech tribe in Ethiopia's Omo Valley women take sole responsibility for everything that happens in the dwelling. The Dassanech live in *miede*, semicircular constructions with no interior divisions that are made with sticks and branches. These are built primarily by women, and it is their task to maintain them. The first item placed in the *miede* after it has been erected is a small, skeletal structure made from reeds and rope. It is used to store valuable items such as tobacco and coffee. Within the hut, the woman's area is on the right-hand side and the man's on the left.

In Kenya, the loaf-shaped or circular houses, *inkajijik,* of the Masai are built by women. Timber poles are fixed directly in the ground and interwoven with a lattice of smaller branches, which is plastered with a mixture of mud, sticks, grass, cow dung, urine, and ash. The loaf-shaped houses are about 3m (10ft) wide, 5m (16½ft) long, and just over a metre (yard) high. They are grouped to form villages, which are in turn enclosed by circular thorn fences that protect the Masai and their livestock from wild animals and raiders. Building them is the men's task.

The women are also responsible for making the ritual houses for the *manyatta*, a circle of huts, made of cow dung and branches, built on a sacred site. This is where the *eunoto* – the Masai initiation rite that signifies the passage of male youths to adulthood – takes place (*see* Circumcision and Separation, page 160). As a sign of respect, the women whose sons are taking part in the ritual construct its most important building: the *osingira*. Much work goes into preparing its exterior, but the inside is the powerful space; it is where the young men are blessed by the senior elders, who invoke Enkai, the Masai deity, to protect them.

> ## The loaf-shaped or circular houses, *inkajijik*, of the Masai are built by women.

Dogon villages

Dogon villages, in the dry, sandy desert of Mali, are laid out in the shape of the human body. Just as the tribe's family houses symbolize the female body (*see* page 74), a village represents a human figure lying on its back, orientated from north to south. The men's council house where decisions are taken is in the "head", the northernmost part, and is surrounded by carvings of human figures. The round lodges on the east and west, where women live/are confined when they are menstruating, are the "hands". The *ginna*, tiny houses in which the families live, represent the chest and belly. Stones to crush oil and the foundation altar symbolize the female and male genitals respectively, and are in the centre of the village. At the south are the communal altars – the "feet".

Inside and outside

The Islamic requirement that wives should not display their beauty to men other than their husband and close family members has affected architecture in Arabic Africa, which shows a clear distinction between the inside, which is a private, female area, and the outside, a public, male area. The houses of the Hausa tribe of northern Nigeria are made of red, laterite soil, rich in clay, and are clustered in walled compounds around a central palace, mosque, and market. Narrow, winding footpaths thread their way around the walls, which can be forbiddingly high depending on the number of buildings they enclose. Each compound has a single entrance hut; generally, only kinsmen are allowed to pass through this. A male visitor is not allowed to go beyond the *shigifa*, the inner entrance, through which only husbands are allowed.

The buildings are noted for their elaborate mud facades. These usually surround only the doorway of the entrance hut, although prosperous Hausas draw attention to their houses by decorating the entire facade with bas-relief arabesques and contrasting colours. The non-representational art of Islam is combined with bold motifs of familiar objects such as swords, guns, and bicycles. This creates an attractive barrier that marks the boundary between inside and outside.

Tribal "town planning"

Tribal homes are positioned according to a coherent design, which often organizes the village according to kinship groups. In West Africa, the camps of the nomadic Fulani are temporary, but where the tents are placed follows a definite pattern. Each son of the chief is considered to be the head of his own lineage, and the family of the most senior son pitches its tents furthest to the west; that of the most junior one is positioned furthest to the east. In this way, the seniority of each family is instantly revealed to visitors.

Opposite: Baka children outside houses in the rainforest of the Republic of Congo. Women are responsible for building the huts, which are made of plant materials; large rainforest leaves are used for waterproofing.

During fieldwork in the Trobriand Islands south-east of New Guinea, carried out from 1915 to 1918, the Polish anthropologist Bronislaw Malinowski observed that villages were organized in two concentric circles. The outer ring contained family dwelling houses and the inner ring consisted of ceremonial yam houses. A street ran between the circles. Great prestige was associated with horticultural success, and the houses in which yams, the islanders' main crop, were stored were even more carefully constructed than family homes. The carved and adorned boards on their exteriors were decorated with mythical animals. The innermost space – the land encircled by the yam houses – included the burial and dancing grounds, and was where ceremonies were held. All the buildings in the village faced this area.

Environmental housing

The design of tribal houses, and how they are constructed, depends on a region's geographical features, its climate, and the availability of materials. The homes of the Berbers of Matmata in southern Tunisia are deep in the desert soil to provide escape from the intense summer heat: six or more underground rooms lead from a large, crater-like courtyard. This is big enough to fill the rooms with light and fresh air, and is reached through a sloping tunnel.

In Ethiopia, the Dassanech have recently developed a contemporary way to deal with the gruelling desert heat: huts have curved, corrugated-iron roofs that reflect back some of the intensity of the sun's heat. They are also extremely well ventilated, with gaps close to the ground that allow air to flow through the building. In contrast, the Miskito of coastal Honduras live high up in log stilt houses, to protect themselves from flooding. Stilt houses are also used by other tribal peoples around the world, such as the Warao of Venezuela who live on the banks of the Amazon, and by coastal and river-dwelling tribes on the islands of the central and South Pacific; examples are the Abelam of New Guinea and some Maori groups in New Zealand.

Building with trees

Building with leaves and branches has a long tradition: traces of human shelter, made from trees and believed to date from 400,000 years ago, have been found

in Terra Amata in southern France. A more modern example is the Babongo tribe of Gabon, whose traditional huts, *tudi,* are constructed entirely with materials gathered from the hot and humid rainforest. The basic skeletal structure is made with a flexible sapling that is bent into a curved shape and overlaid with flat, wide leaves that help to keep the hut waterproof. Camps consist of six to eight huts, which can house up to 20 people.

The Baka pygmies are hunter-gatherers who live in the rainforest areas of Cameroon, Congo, and the Central African Republic. They are traditionally nomadic and live in *mongulu,* family houses made of branches and leaves. The women are responsible for building the huts, and make the most of the natural rainforest resources that are essential to the tribe's cultural and spiritual survival. They use flexible, thin branches to construct a semicircular framework, then weave fresh leaves through this to make the basic, dome-shaped structure. Other plant materials are added to make the hut more compact and waterproof.

However, these traditional homes are threatened by increasing pressure on forest resources by logging companies and farming communities. The World Wildlife Fund, recognizing that the best way to protect forests is to protect the rights of the people who live in them, has recommended that the Baka's access to conserved areas should be increased, allowing them to gather food in national parks, so that they can continue to live within the rainforest as they have for generations.

Yak wool: a blessed material

High in the Bhutanese Himalayas, building materials are few and far between. When men from the Layap tribe take their yak herds across the mountains to pasture, they create temporary satellite camps with tents made from large pieces of tightly woven yak hair. The yak wool seems to defy the laws of physics: natural light enters, and smoke escapes, through large holes in the weaving, yet the tents are waterproof. The Layaps believe that yak wool is blessed, and say this is what gives it its extraordinary qualities.

> The Layaps believe that yak wool is blessed, and say this is what gives it its extraordinary qualities.

Mud, glorious mud

Mud – unbaked, raw earth sometimes mixed with oil or water – is a strong and adaptable building material, and has been used for sultan's palaces and mosques in the Middle East, baroque churches in Peru, and eight-storey houses in south Yemen. It can be used to build entire rural villages or to create shelters for the urban poor. At the start of the 1980s, more than one-third of the world's population lived in raw earth houses and it is likely that the earliest cities of Mesopotamia were built entirely of this material. In Africa, Djenne, in what is now Mali, was an important trading centre for gold and salt on the trans-Saharan route, and housed a large and wealthy merchant class. Typically, their houses had sweeping vertical buttresses moulded from mud made with vegetable oil. In France, at least 15 per cent of buildings are made of raw earth with examples surviving near Grenoble, Toulouse, Rennes, Avignon, and Chartres. The Great Wall of China, large parts of which are mud, has lasted since the 3rd century BC – a testament to the durability of the material.

Top left: Multistorey mud skyscrapers built 500 years ago tower above the desert in Shibam, Yemen.

Bottom left: In Togo, two men build a *tata* by tossing balls of mud to add to the structure layer by layer. The *tata* is a secure, two-storey family home shaped like a fortress with two towers. The ground floor is used for cooking and to house animals; the top floor is exposed to the sky and used for sleeping and keeping watch. Both of the towers open to provide ample storage for grain.

Above: The Great Mosque of Djenne, Mali, is the world's largest mudbrick building. It has been designated a UNESCO World Heritage Site.

Ancient and modern

Building with earth is a continuous tradition. An example is the rectangular mudbrick and timber houses in the villages of the Anatolian region of Turkey, which have hardly changed since the Neolithic period. In other parts of the world, however, new technology has led to changes in traditional styles. Tin has great prestige as a roofing material in parts of Africa, for example among the Hausa of Nigeria, where it is rapidly replacing thatch. Although a tin roof is hot in summer, cold in winter, and noisy when it rains, it requires less maintenance than one made with leaves and branches.

Today, modern techniques make home building in urbanized and industrialized societies a complicated process, one in which the house owner may have very little direct participation. Designs and fashions evolve constantly and the symbolic meaning of homes, how they are constructed, and the way in which space is used differ across the world. However, such differences cannot take away from the fact that the need for shelter is at the very centre of the human experience. No matter where we may be on the planet, home is where we come together.

Top left: A one-storey mud house in Morocco provides much-needed shade from the relentless sun.

Bottom left: Houses in the Ethiopian city of Harar are designed to stay as cool as possible. Ventilation is maintained by wood-framed windows and the houses are painted with light colours to reflect heat.

Top centre: In Buniamin, Syria, conical mud huts provide private spaces around a communal area.

Top right: The Gurunsi of Burkina Faso paint their adobe houses in an annual festival. Here, a chief's compound shows a typically colourful geometric decoration.

Bottom centre: In Oku, Cameroon, a woman enters a traditional house made from mud reinforced with carved bamboo and hardwood.

4 Courtship and Marriage

Some form of marriage is an essential human institution. It has maintained stable social relationships in, and between, communities throughout recorded history. The specific form of marriage varies – it can be a monogamous love match, a polygamous arranged marriage, or a purely civil contract – and the courtship rituals and customs that lead to it are also widely diverse. Marriage seems to be a universal aspect of being human. It plays such an important role in our lives that ceremonies to celebrate it are traditionally linked to religious and magical rites.

What is marriage?

Marriage is a public ritual that defines the movement of people between families. It is a contract that entails economic responsibilities. It is also an open, public declaration that two lovers belong to each other, and that nobody should interfere with their relationship. Even in modern, industrialized societies where being married is not a legal or moral prerequisite for a couple to have a family, many people choose to make this declaration, whether they are atheist or religious, straight or gay. After years of detailed comparison of the role marriage plays in tribes around the world, most anthropologists define it as a form of contract

for the production and maintenance of children. Almost without exception it is a woman's husband who is the legal father of her child, whether he is the genetic father or not.

The rules of attraction

Certain body types convey a subconscious message about the desirability of another person as a potential mate. Put simply, a large part of what attracts two people to each other comes from an inbuilt desire to produce healthy children. Researchers at the University of Texas found that winners of the Miss America beauty contest averaged a waist-to-hip ratio of 0.7: the waist was exactly 0.7 times the size of the hips. This "hourglass" figure is an indicator of a woman's fitness and ability to bear children, and the researchers found that in the United States the perceived attractiveness of women with this ratio holds true over a range of body weights and types. In South Africa, Ndebele brides wear immense, beaded hoops around their legs and hips to exaggerate the voluptuous body that the men of the tribe admire, perhaps because this shape suggests that a woman has enough fat stores to nourish a baby successfully throughout pregnancy and during breast-feeding.

Women are also on the look-out for indications of biological fitness in potential mates. The men of the Surma tribe of Ethiopia paint their bodies to emphasize their musculature when they exhibit their masculine strength in the *donga*, a ritual in which they fight each other brutally with sticks. Combatants are often injured, sometimes severely, but the women of the tribe find battle scars attractive as they are indicative of a man who has strength and endurance. Woodabe men of Niger perform annual ceremonies to display their strength; painted and decorated, they dance in a circle and wear beading around their legs and arms to exaggerate their muscles. In both

Previous page:
Abdasi brides and grooms in India carry earthen posts on their heads and shoulders during a mass marriage ceremony on the outskirts of Siliguri. The ceremony saw the wedding of 100 couples from the nearby areas of north Bengal.

Opposite: A Zulu wedding procession in South Africa.

Right: A Kosovan bride in the village of Donje Ljubinje in the Shar mountains between Kosovo and Macedonia. The bride's face is lavishly painted to prevent bad luck and her handmade dress and headdress are decorated with intricate beading. This type of traditional wedding has become a proud symbol of local identity.

cases the men exhibit qualities that show their fitness and suggest that they would father strong, healthy children.

The scent of sexual attraction

Scientists have begun to piece together ideas about what causes two specific people to be attracted to each other. They suggest that, as everyone's genetic code is unique, each individual is looking for a partner whose type of genes would best combine with theirs – someone who is genetically fit for them. Recent research has shown that smell is an essential part of physical attraction, and that we are attracted to the smell of some people more than others.

Scientists suggest that each person has a scent that is attractive only to people with whom they are likely to have healthy offspring. It has been known for some time that pheromones (aromatic molecules secreted by the body) can trigger obvious sexual responses in animals, and it seems that humans are no different. The latest research suggests that we have a "vomeronasal organ", which receives pheromone molecules and is supposedly directly connected to a part of the brain responsible for emotions.

To determine whether women could differentiate between men with similar and dissimilar immune systems to theirs on the basis of smell alone, Claus Wedekind of the Zoological Institute at Bern conducted an experiment in which women were asked to rate the pleasantness and sexiness of students' sweaty T-shirts, and the intensity of their reactions to them. It was found that women "who are dissimilar to a particular male's MHC [Major Histocompatibility Complex – immune system markers of identity] perceive his odour as more pleasant than women whose MHC is more similar to that of the test man". In simple terms, they found that men who were genetically dissimilar to themselves more attractive, probably because these are the men with whom they were most likely to have healthy offspring.

A study by Dr Carole Ober of the University of Chicago's Department of Human Genetics showed similar results. DNA samples were taken from South Dakotan Hutterites. An isolated religious group whose members tend to marry among themselves and have large families, the Hutterites can be seen as being analogous to a tribal band in a remote area. They are descended from only 64 European immigrants to the United States, so they all have a similar genetic make-up, including immune system types.

Hutterite couples gave biological samples to the researchers, and the matches of MHC immune system markers were examined and compared with the matches in random pairings (based on genetic data generated by a computer simulation). The law of averages predicted that there would be many more Hutterite couples with similar immune systems (and therefore genetic similarity) than there were in reality.

It is suggested that the aromatic pheromones that their bodies secreted could have prevented men and women with immune systems that were too similar being attracted to each other.

All this adds an intriguing new layer to the reasons for tribal rituals. The annual dance of the Woodabe of Niger involves the men dancing for hours, sweating. The women are expected to inspect them, and stand close to them, and can touch those to whom they are attracted. A woman is allowed to choose a partner with whom she can have sexual intercourse that evening. It could be argued that tribal courtship rituals such as this dance enable potential mates to meet and touch, and become physically close so that they increase their chances of producing healthy offspring by selecting a partner whose smell they find attractive.

Beauty: in the eye of the beholder

Mate selection is, of course, also determined by cultural concepts of beauty; a petite woman considered beautiful in France may be regarded as ugly by the Igbo of Nigeria who find tall, large women attractive, and consider long, thin limbs in a girl to be a characteristic of great female beauty. Until

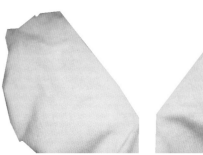

recently, the Igbo practised *ino na nkpul*: a prospective wife stayed in a "fattening" hut before her marriage, where she was fed as much possible, with little opportunity to exercise. As a general rule, the Igbo do not find overweight girls with stout limbs attractive, as they are unlikely to grow taller, but for other tribes in Niger and Nigeria fat is beautiful. Djerma women compete to see which of them can put on the most weight at a festival called *hangandi*, that involves a beauty contest. They train for this by gorging on food, especially millet, and drinking lots of water. The heaviest woman is declared the winner and given a prize, as well as more food. Why people find each other attractive can therefore be explained partly by science and partly by culture – but also by personality, past experiences, and sexuality, all of which can lead to extremes of desire and emotion.

> Scientists suggest that each person has a scent that is attractive only to people with whom they are likely to have healthy offspring.

Lovesickness

For the Achuar of the Amazonian region, lovesickness is a pathological condition, described as a type of melancholy that has been caused by a malevolent shaman. It mainly affects young people – men or women, regardless of whether or not they are married. The victim sinks into depression and self-disgust, and is seized by the desire to commit suicide, particularly at dusk. Afflicted men are described as weeping silently – convinced, for example, that their new young wife does not love them. Since a shaman caused the illness, the

The demands of beauty

Among the Padaung of Myanmar and Thailand, a long neck is associated with female beauty. It is achieved by placing brass rings around a girl's neck when she is five, and adding to them throughout her childhood. Because this is done gradually, her body adapts to them and her nervous system is not damaged. Eventually, the entire length of her neck is adorned with silver chains and coins that signal elegance, wealth, and status. The ideal number of rings is around 37.

The lotus foot in China (*see* pages 43–4 and page 46) was considered to be exceptionally attractive by Chinese, but reviled in other societies as mutilation. The practice of scarification by the Nuba of Sudan (*see* page 163) and lip plugs among the Mursi of Ethiopia (*see* page 166) are also examples of cultural concepts of beauty.

only way to cure this affliction is via the help of another shaman who performs rituals to rid the lovesick man of the spirits that are causing his melancholy.

Forbidden love

Even in the sexually permissive West, there are restrictions on both marriage and erotic love. In Britain, sexual intercourse is illegal before the age of 16. In Spain, however, it is legal between 13-year-olds. In Afghanistan, a man must be 18 before he can have heterosexual sex, and a woman must be married and have sex only with her husband. Homosexual sex is illegal in Afghanistan, parts of the Caribbean, Fiji, Bangladesh, and scores of other countries.

Incest is universally prohibited, and carries with it the kind of horror that led Oedipus to blind himself in shame. There is no tribe that does not abhor it, but incest is defined very differently across the world. Every society rules against its members having sex with, or marrying, certain family members – but who these members are differs. Unions between parents and children are forbidden almost the world over, though instances of sex between mothers and sons have been recorded among the Caribs and Inuit. Brother–sister unions were known among the kings of Hawaii, the royal families of the Inca and Egyptians, and the ancient Irish.

"Honour killings" are an extreme example of what can happen when a girl rebels against her culture's rules on marriage. According to the United Nations, at least 5000 women a year are killed worldwide by relatives who believe they have disgraced the family name by refusing to marry the man who has been chosen for them. The women may be in love with someone else, or simply not want to marry the partner selected for them. The brutal murder of Du' Khalil Awad, a 17-year-old from the Yazidi of Iraqi Kurdistan, who was stoned to death in 2007 for falling in love with a boy outside her tribe, is, tragically, not uncommon.

Family relationships

The following terms describe specific types of kinship, and how families within tribes relate to each other.

Patrilineal: A family that traces its descent along the male line – through the husband's father and paternal grandfather. Many African tribes, such as the Nuer of East Africa, organize families into patrilineal descent groups, and people are often able to recite the names of their male ancestors.

Matrilineal: A family that traces its descent along the female line – through the wife's mother and maternal grandmother. This is common in the "matrilineal belt" of tribes across central Africa, and in Asia and the South Pacific; the Trobriand Islanders, south-east of New Guinea, are just one example of many matrilineal tribes.

In many matrilineal societies, the husband is economically superfluous to his wife, who gets everything she needs from her brothers and other close family members. Among the Hopi of Arizona, women own rooms in the village and hand them down to their daughters. Men regard sisters'

houses as their real homes and leave their important ritual belongings there. Only everyday objects are taken to a wife's house.

Patrilocal: A bride lives with her husband and his family, and children are brought up in his place of birth. This is the most common form of residence for tribal families around the world.

Matrilocal: The husband joins his wife at her mother's house. Sometimes he just visits her and lives with his mother and siblings at their family home.

Exogamous: A tribe in which marriage partners must be from different descent groups.

Endogamous: A tribe in which marriage partners must be from the same descent group.

Genitor: The biological father of a child.

Pater: The socially recognized father of a child. The social and biological fathers are often the same man, as in the West. But this is not always the case, as shown by the Nayar (see page 96) and Nuer (see page 97).

Opposite left: A Khasi couple pose in traditional wedding costume after their wedding ceremony. The Khasi are a matrilineal society in north-east India; they trace their descent through their mothers and take their maternal ancestors' surnames.

Opposite centre: The Minangkabau of Sumatra are considered the world's largest matrilineal society; property is passed down from mothers to daughters.

Opposite right: A Miao wedding ceremony in China's Guizhou Province. The patrilineal Miao live in villages based on local lineages, and can often trace their ancestry back into the past through several generations.

So around the globe, and in tribal cultures in particular, men and women do not always have the freedom to choose their sexual partner or who they will marry.

There are three main ways in which a person obtains a partner to marry. They may follow tradition and marry a specific category of person, the marriage may be arranged by a couple's parents, or, as generally happens in industralized societies, they may choose a marriage partner freely and spontaneously. Different rules apply in different cultures.

At least 5000 women a year are killed worldwide by relatives who believe they have disgraced the family name by refusing to marry the man who has been chosen for them.

Arranged marriages

In some tribes, marriages are arranged when the future husband and wife are children. In the 19th century, in *The History of Human Marriage*, Edward Westermarck, an explorer and early anthropologist, described how Inuits north of Churchill in Alaska promised baby girls to teenage boys: "as soon as a girl is born, the young lad who wishes to have her for a wife goes to her father's tent and proffers himself. If accepted, a promise is given which is considered binding, and the girl is delivered to her betrothed at the proper age." The Ashanti of Ghana are reported to arrange betrothals when a baby is in the womb, promising it to a grown male suitor if it is a girl. The promise is revoked if the child is a boy.

Infant betrothals are also practised by the Kadara grain farmers of Nigeria. When a girl is born, a man in the village approaches her father to arrange a later marriage, the father accepts him, and the engagement is symbolized by an exchange of beer. When the girl is between three and six years old, her fiancé starts to work on her father's farm, at first for only for a couple of days each year.

He must also give annual gifts of salt to the mother of the bride-to-be. After he has worked on the farm for 10 years, increasing the time he spends there by a day or so every year, he may demand his bride – who will then be between 13 and 16. She moves to his house and a marriage ceremony is performed. Despite the engagement, no value is set on premarital chastity and it is fairly common for the girl to be already pregnant. If this is the case, she is welcomed into the lineage of her new husband's family and her pregnancy is prized as proof of her fertility. If, once the 10 years have been reached, the girl refuses to marry her fiancé, she is allowed to select another husband from his patrilineage. However, if she rejects this alternative partner, her father has to provide a substitute for her – usually her sister.

Prescribed marriages

Some tribes don't arrange marriages, but have strict rules about who is, and who is not, an acceptable partner. In endogamous tribes, such as the Korku of central India, members of a lineage or clan have to marry within their descent group. In exogamous tribes, such as the Trobriand Islanders, south-east of New Guinea, they must find a partner outside their lineage. The rules are strictly enforced because the links that marriage alliances create between lineages are important in maintaining the peace in a tribe.

In other tribes, an individual has no choice as to whom they marry. The most common form of this prescribed marriage is cousin marriage, where a person is expected to marry their first cousin on a particular side of the family; for example, members of the Tonga tribe in Zambia are expected to marry their father's sister's child. The result is that people move from one family to another, in a specific direction between lineages, and property moves in the opposite direction in the form of a cattle payment, known as bridewealth. This

> When a girl is born, a man in the village approaches her father to arrange a later marriage, the father accepts him, and the engagement is symbolized by an exchange of beer.

leads to a chain of exchange between descent groups where people receive marriage partners from one group and cattle from another. In this way an alliance system is established across the tribe.

Cousin marriage does not always happen. Sometimes a father's sister doesn't have a child, or the betrothed couple don't want to marry each other. But the rule is an ideal that a tribe as a whole aspires to; in the absence of a biological cousin, a person often marries their social cousin, who is always from the appropriate descent group.

Marriage payments

Before a marriage is finalized, payments are made between families. Like the Tonga of Zambia, the cattle-owning tribes of eastern Africa, such as the Nuer, trace their descent groups through their fathers and grandfathers, and make their payments in the form of bridewealth. Any children born to a Nuer couple belong to the father's lineage, so at marriage the husband's family pays a number of cattle to the woman's family. Interestingly, this is the same number that is paid to a family to compensate it for a murder, providing it with the resources to arrange a marriage for another son, and create a new member of the lineage (a child) to fill the murdered man's place. As the Nuer are polygamous, a man may pay bridewealth more than once, and to do so he must either acquire cattle himself, or use those his family has acquired through his sisters' marriages.

Different types of bridewealth are used by the matrilineal tribes of central Africa, who trace their decent through their mothers and grandmothers. Among the Bemba of north-east Zambia, payment is usually in the form of services. The husband helps his wife's family, particularly with farming, gives them presents of drink, and pays for the wedding; because the family is matrilocal, the wife remains with her mother and siblings who provide the resources to raise any children of the union. There is no need, in this instance, to compensate the bride's family as she and her children will benefit them economically. The bridewealth exists to ensure smooth relations between in-laws.

Below: Two Nuer women in Ethiopia on their wedding day. They have married the same man and are now co-wives.

Daughters and dowries

Islam prescribes that to make a marriage legal a man must provide his bride with a "dower" – a gift that becomes her own personal property. Perhaps to ease social relations, presents are also often given to her parents.

A Hindu father, on the other hand, offers his daughter as a bride and gives a dowry to the bridegroom's family. The Chenchus, a food-gathering Hindu tribe of the Andhra Pradesh forests in south-east India, practise the ancient marriage traditions. After the father has given a dowry, he continues to send presents to the family, and must also provide for the wedding feast, which is usually worth more than the dowry. Elsewhere in India, the amount of

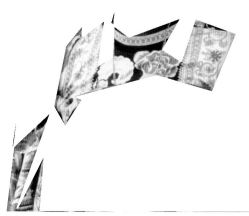

money a Hindu father gives depends on the bridegroom's caste. Each Hindu caste is further divided into subcastes, ranked in order of superiority. The ideal is for a girl to marry into the subcaste above her own. Among the Sinhalese people of Sri Lanka, no dowry is paid if the bride marries into her own subcaste, but her family is expected to pay if she marries above it. Just as people are prepared to spend extra on a status-raising car, families may pay more for a marriage that enhances their social standing.

The dowry is sometimes interpreted as "paying" a family to take a daughter, but most anthropologists dispute this. In actuality, the girl herself benefits from the money as it goes with her to her new family. It is paid with a daughter and not a son because, in this system, the son inherits money whereas the daughter does not. In a sense, it is a way for her family to compensate her for her lack of inheritance.

> Just as people are prepared to spend extra on a status-raising car, families may pay more for a marriage that enhances their social standing.

Polygamous marriages

Although monogamy is statistically the most frequently occurring type of marriage, polygamy has been recorded in peoples around the world. It can be divided into polygyny, where a man takes many wives, and polyandry, where a woman takes many husbands.

Men with many wives

In Africa, as in other parts of the world, polygyny is usually the privilege of the wealthy. A man takes many wives to increase his power, prestige, and alliances with other kin groups. Whereas the Qur'an limits the number of wives to four, there are societies in which a limitless number can be taken.

In some tribes the standing of the wives in a polygynous marriage varies. The Xhosa of southern Africa classify theirs in the order in which they marry them, giving special status to the first three. A Swazi husband can promote a wife married later in life above his other wives only if she is high-ranking. In other societies and tribes wives are ostensibly equal. The Qur'an states that the same amount of love and support must be given to each wife. Similarly, in the polygynous households of the Achuar of the Amazonian rainforest, whose marriages are arranged by families, the husband is expected to scrupulously respect each wife's turn to spend time with him and have sex with him. If this is the case, the wives are expected to be modest and sexually passive, and to work harmoniously together and with their husband. If a wife is neglected, she will make her desires explicit.

Below: Bridegroom Milton Mbhele with his four brides, left to right, Happiness, Thobile, Simgele, and Zanele at their wedding near Ladysmith, South Africa, in 2009. South African law recognizes traditional polygamous marriages, which remain common among the Zulu and Swazi, but it is rare for the weddings to occur simultaneously.

Women with many husbands

Polyandry is documented in some tribes around the world. In the 19th century, the Nayar of southern India practised

Mswati III of Swaziland

In Swaziland in southern Africa, a king is expected to marry a woman from every clan in order to cement relationships with each part of the country. This means that he must have many wives. The first two are chosen for him by national councillors. They have specific roles in rituals and their sons can never claim the throne. The first wife must be a member of the Matsebula clan, and the second must be a Motsa.

An independent council, the *Liqoqo*, decides which of the king's other wives will be the Great Wife and which the Queen Mother. The son of the Great Wife becomes the next king, provided he is her only son and she is of good character – he cannot be the heir to the throne if his mother is not of good standing. The king can marry a fiancée only after she has fallen pregnant, proving she can bear an heir. Until then, she is a *liphovela*, or bride. In 2007, Mswati III, Swaziland's king and one of the world's last absolute monarchs, had 13 wives. In September 2008, he chose his 14th wife.

Mswati, like his predecessors, chooses his wives at the *umhlanga*, or reed dance, which was traditionally simply an opportunity for Swaziland's maidens to pay tribute to the Queen Mother. Every year the country's virgins – recently as many as 100,000 – gather in the capital, Mbabane, to perform the dance before a royal audience. They bring reeds that they present to the Queen Mother and use to build windbreaks around her residence. Ceremonies last for a week and on the last day, wearing only skirts, the girls sing while they parade and dance before the royal family.

Right: Swaziland's King Mswati III points at maidens during the annual *umhlanga*, or reed dance, at the royal residence near Mbabane. Mswati, who already has over a dozen wives, has caused controversy by using the reed dance, which is traditionally held to honour the Queen Mother, as an opportunity to select a new bride.

Bottom left: Swazi maidens bear reeds for the Queen Mother during the annual *umhlanga*.

Below: Princess Sikhanyiso Dlamini, the first-born daughter of Mswati III, dances in the *umhlanga* procession. The ceremony has become one of the most important festivities in the country, and thousands of maidens from across Swaziland take part.

polyandrous marriage. Before a girl reached puberty, a man performed the *tali* rite, in which he tied a ribbon around her throat, and they were ritually married. The ceremony had to take place before a girl reached puberty or, in some extreme cases where her family couldn't conceal her maturity, her kinsmen killed her to avoid the shame of having a girl who was unable to marry in their family. The *tali* husband had the right to deflower the girl, and their relationship could later develop into an ongoing sexual one. However, this did not have to be the case: the *tali* bride's only obligation was to honour her husband by observing certain funeral rites for him when he died. She lived with her matrilineal family, and once she was mature she took a small number of visiting husbands, who were outside her lineage but were normally from the same Hindu caste. When one of them came to see her, he placed his weapons outside her door, to avoid being surprised by another husband. The visiting husband always arrived after supper and left before breakfast.

> The *tali* bride's only obligation was to honour her husband by observing certain funeral rites for him when he died.

If the woman became pregnant, one of the husbands, not necessarily the child's biological father, accepted paternity, covered all the delivery expenses, and offered gifts to the midwife who attended the birth. This man was the child's social father, or pater. If no husband accepted paternity rights, it was assumed that the woman had had relations with a man of a lower caste or, appallingly, with a Muslim or Christian. In this case, the strictest matrilineal kinsmen could exert their right to kill the woman, a fate the child would probably have shared. If her kinsmen were more lenient, they might expel her from her caste and lineage, and perform funeral rites as if she had died.

Left: Polygamy is practised by Uighur tribes in China. This family of one husband, two wives, and six children is preparing to eat outside its house in Xinjiang Province.

The husband and father provided gifts, but did not maintain his wife and child, who received all they needed from their matrilineal group (their mother's family). If the husband ceased having a sexual relationship with the woman, he also stopped giving her gifts. As an individual, he had no rights in the upbringing of his child, but he had an important role in legitimizing his or her birth. He would also be polygynous, and have a number of wives whom he would visit.

Another, less complicated system of polyandry is practised among the Kadara of Nigeria. A married woman can run away with another man who has prearranged the elopement with her father. The man must then send a series of gifts to her father, and when this gift-giving is complete, he is accepted as the woman's new husband. She now has two husbands. She may live with only one of them at a time, but is permitted to change her residence whenever she wants to.

Unusual relationships

Polygamy has been described as multiple monogamy, and most polygamous unions are more similar to monogamous ones than might first appear. Two individuals make a contract to marry, but one or both of them can also make this contract with other people, generally to increase wealth, social importance, and the number of children. However, there are instances where the rights to a wife belong to a group of men rather than one man. Among the Nuer of Sudan and Ethiopia, a husband can give his kin sexual access to his wife. Among the neighbouring Lo Dagaa tribe, if the junior of male twins is unmarried, he has rights to his brother's wife.

Another Nuer practice is the "ghost marriage": if a man dies before he becomes a father, a close kinsman marries a wife "to his name". Children of this union take the name of the dead man, who is therefore recognized as one of their ancestors. If the kinsman is unable to acquire the bridewealth to make another marriage, to his own name, or if he dies before he is able to do so, another kinsman should make a ghost marriage on his behalf.

The Nuer also have a type of union that Evans Pritchard, an anthropologist who studied the tribe in the 1930s, described as woman-to-woman marriage. A woman, typically one who is barren, and who is often a diviner or procurer of medicine, chooses a bride from an appropriate lineage. She has her own wealth, often through healing, and pays the bridewealth with her own cattle so that she can marry her wife. From then on she is a female husband, and chooses a man to live with her wife, in order to have sex with her and hopefully impregnate her; the two women are not sexual partners. If the female husband is herself married, the man may be one of her husband's relatives. The children the wife bears take the name of the female husband. This means that a woman with wealth in land and palms is able to found a compound and establish control over people, to create an estate for an heir. She can take as many wives as she can afford and remains head of the compound until her death. This type of marriage has been recorded in more than 30 African tribes, including the Zulu of southern Africa and the Yoruba of Nigeria.

> There are instances where the rights to a wife belong to a group of men rather than one man.

Widow inheritance

Levirate marriages, where a man marries his brother's widow, are also practised by the Nuer; they were, incidentally, part of the culture of the Israelites of the Old Testament. If a man dies, his brother is expected to inherit his wife, suggesting that the matrimonial bonds between the families outlast death. The Kadara of Nigeria take this family obligation even further, and a man may be expected to marry the wife of his paternal or maternal grandfather if he dies. Among the Mossi of Burkina Faso in western Africa, a son is expected to inherit his father's wives (but not his own mother) and his advancement in the community depends on his father's death as he is of lower status until he marries. Mossi fathers are reported to be so sensitive about being replaced by their sons that they act as if they resent their growth, especially that of the first son. A son must not have sex with his father's wives during his father's lifetime.

The fight against Aids

Because of the tragic prevalence of HIV in Africa, people in African communities are trying to stop the practice of widow inheritance, which can spread the virus across generations and through entire families. In East Africa, infidelity and forced marriages are also the focus of attempts to prevent Aids devastating communities. The Swahili saying, "It is better to have a still curtain hanging inside the house than a flag blowing to and fro outside the house" means that it is better to have one partner (comparable to the curtain in the proverb) than to go back and forth (like a flag in the wind) between different partners.

Is virginity important?

In some tribes, such as the Chenchus of India and the Berbers of North Africa, it is necessary for a couple to wait until they are married before they have sex, and female virginity is highly prized. In Roman Catholic European countries today, premarital sex remains a sin and chastity a virtue, particularly in women. It is unusual for male virginity to be given such importance, although the Sarakatsani – mountain shepherds of Greece and Bulgaria – regard it highly, and praise chastity in boys.

In other cultures a man would not expect to marry a virgin. In Samoa in the South Pacific, a girl lost her virginity as part of her initiation rites, around the time of her puberty – a practice later banned by American authorities on the island. This was also recorded among central African tribes, where the rites frequently involved ritual defloration; a girl's father instructed a man to have sex with her, and she was not subsequently allowed to have a relationship with him.

Many tribes encourage sexual freedom before marriage. The Trobriand Islanders, as described in the early 20th century by the Polish anthropologist Bronislaw Malinowski, had the freedom to take different lovers throughout their youth. They had a trial and error approach to courtship that seems remarkably similar to that which is followed by many people in industrialized societies today. Malinowski describes them as taking an "experimental" interest in their sexual arrangements and changing their partners. As time went on, their partnerships tended to extend in length and depth, and their ties grew stronger and more permanent. As a rule, couples emerged with a genuine and passionate attachment to each other, usually based on affinity of character. With the consent of the girl's family the two lovers married. Once married, they were expected to remain faithful to each other, as is the norm in industrialized societies.

Above: During an AIDS/HIV awareness campaign in India, Mithun Ghosh dressed as a groom to highlight the importance of blood tests before marriage. Some 2.5 million Indians are living with HIV, and the prevalence of the disease is drastically affecting sex, marriages, and family life, as is also tragically the case on the African continent.

Opposite left: Virgin brides of the Ait Haddidou tribe at a Berber wedding festival in Morocco. Berber society expects both partners, but most importantly the bride, to be virgins at the time of marriage.

Opposite right: A Muria boy in a *gotul* in Bastar, India. A *gotul* is a dormitory where boys and girls sleep, work, and experiment with sex before marriage. Around puberty, Muria children are encouraged to gain sexual experience and form relationships in order to help them select compatible marriage partners later in life.

This freedom of courtship and sexual liaison is found in tribes throughout the world, such as the Akamba of East Africa. And in the tribe-like societies of European peasants during the Middle Ages there was a documented system of trial nights, whereby couples could have sex with each other before betrothal, to see whether they were well suited before they married.

Premarital pregnancy

Although the Trobriand Islanders are tolerant of sex before marriage, they are deeply unimpressed by premarital pregnancy. Young couples avoid having children out of wedlock through both contraception and abortion. A child born to unmarried parents is also a taboo in other tribes that encourage sexual freedom before marriage; in the aristocratic fraternities of Polynesia, the children of such unions faced death unless they were adopted by a married couple.

Alternatively, for the Pueblos of the south-west United States, a child conceived in a premarital union is a blessing, and an omen that encourages the lovers to marry. But they believe that a child needs to be brought up by a married couple, and even if it is conceived out of wedlock it must be born into a marriage.

The wedding ceremony

Symbolism in marriage ceremonies often expresses the continuity of a people. For example, in the West the bride is traditionally accompanied by a small child (or children), and the church or place where the wedding is held is filled with flowers, and sometimes fruit. Similarly, in many tribes there is a symbolic focus on children and fertility. Among the Quechua people of the High Andes, unions involve at least 10 elaborate ceremonies over the course of several years. First, there is a trial marriage. If this goes well the couple become officially betrothed, which is celebrated with both a Quechua and a Roman Catholic ceremony. However, the marriage is not complete until the families have hosted the wedding feast, and performed a ritual where crops are planted and blessed as symbols of the couple's fertility. This last ceremony marks their transition into adulthood, and means that they are ready to bear children.

Another important function of marriage ceremonies is to dramatize the transfer of a person between families. A Christian wedding shows the movement between kin. The bride arrives, veiled, in a ceremonially virginal state, on her father's arm. She leaves, with the veil thrown back, on the arm of her husband.

Ritual conflicts

Although marriage is a celebration of a union, it has the potential for social rupture: people's roles need to change, they must be deferential to new kin, and they have a different position within a family and community. It also has the potential for conflict between families, which is often symbolically expressed in the wedding ceremony, with weeping, miming, capture, or sham fighting. Among the Kwadi of Angola, the groom and his relatives chase the bride and her family into the bush. When the two groups meet, they stage a mock fight, which culminates in the groom's

party snatching the bride and carrying her back into the village, pursued by her family. On the next day, the feasting and dancing commence and the groom provides an ox for slaughter. On the day after that, the bride ritually milks a cow, the food is shared between the families at a large feast, and they are reconciled.

In *Nyoro Marriage and Affinity* (1958) J H M Beatties describes how the Nyoro of Uganda express the conflict between families. The bride's father writes a letter to the father of the groom, which is read out when the girl is first brought to her husband's home: "Take the girl in accordance with the custom of our country. She is now yours and you may scold her and beat her if necessary. Our daughter is yours. She is not strong yet and she has not yet had a husband. She is ignorant of marriage, and her husband's father should advise and instruct her gently. If she quarrels with her husband, or if he is angry and finds fault with her, the dispute should be settled peacefully by her husband's father. She often suffers from an illness of the head and chest and if this sometimes prevents her from working properly do not be angry with her. If she wishes to visit her relatives do not prevent her. If she turns out really badly do not beat her excessively; send her back to us and we will refund the bridewealth. She is not in the habit of visiting casually in other people's houses, nor does she attend beer parties, so if she acquires these bad habits the fault will be yours."

The Swiss missionary and anthropologist Henri Junod reported a ritual among the Tsonga tribe of southern Mozambique and Zimbabwe, which involved a remarkably

frank verbal exchange between families when a betrothal was announced. The bride's relatives made a few less than friendly remarks towards the groom's family, including screaming "'You dogs! People of no consequence!'" and informing him that he is a "'Wild beast!'" and they have "'come to cut off his tail and make a man of him.'" Not to be outdone, the family of the groom shout insults at the bride when she arrives in their home: "'Do not steal any longer!', 'Forsake your bad ways and become a good girl.'" This type of exchange is a useful safety valve – a way of expressing a hostile sentiment in a context where it is required to be treated as a joke.

Above: A bride travels by horseback to meet her groom in a traditional Galicnik ceremony in Macedonia. The European custom of veiling is akin to the widespread tradition of secluding the bride before marriage.

Secluding the bride

Brides are often hidden before or after the marriage, a practice that is reflected in the Western tradition of veiling the bride during the first part of the wedding ceremony. Among the Ndembu of Zambia, a girl attains womanhood when she marries, so the ceremony marks her coming of age as well as her union with her husband. Before it is held, she must lie at the bottom of a sacred tree covered with blankets, motionless and hidden, for a whole day. Before she performs this rite she is a girl; afterwards she is on her way to becoming a woman.

A bride's seclusion can last far longer than a day. For a Nyakyusa girl in Tanzania , separation from her community lasts for three months, during which she stays in a hut and does not work in the fields. This is the least physically strenuous time of her life and she is expected to put on weight. At the end of her seclusion, the girl is washed all over with medicated water, the leaves on which she has slept are thrown out of the hut and burned, her hair is shaved, and she jumps over a fire; all this signifies that she is crossing the boundary between two phases of her life.

Conception and birth

Conception can be explained in a variety of ways. In Western society there is the accepted scientific explanation, but there is also the Christian belief in impregnation by a deity and a virgin birth. The Achuar of the Amazon believe that the father deposits a tiny "egg" from his semen in the mother's uterus. He must fortify and feed this egg throughout its gestation, particularly during the last few months, by regularly contributing sperm. The woman is seen purely as providing the environment in which it grows – if the couple are infertile, she is blamed for being unable to provide one that is hospitable. For the Mossi of Burkina Faso, a child born to a man's wife is unquestionably his, even if he has been away from her for years.

Most tribal women give birth within the community, assisted either by their mother and sisters or by a specialist midwife in the village. In North American tribes, the midwife traditionally prepared herbal remedies – the root of the blue cohosh was used to speed the birth – and delivered the child. The practice of *couvade* is scattered around the globe: at the time of the birth the husband mimics the physiological disabilities of his wife. He swoons, goes to bed, is swaddled, and demands care. The wife rises from childbirth, assumes her duties, and looks after her husband and the newborn child. *Couvade* could be interpreted as either a selfish act on the part of the husband or as a touching gesture of solidarity.

Bringing up children

Just as Western children learn the values of their societies at school as well as at home, tribal children are socialized by the wider community even when they are cared for within the husband and wife family unit. An Achuar father is affectionate and caring towards a baby, bouncing it on his knees and cuddlling and embracing it. But once it begins to walk he is usually more restrained. A child looks up to its father as an imposing disciplinary figure, and receives affection from the women of the tribe.

Opposite: Hazara women in rural areas of Afghanistan usually give birth at home. Here, a midwife checks a pregnant woman. Pregnancy and childbirth are exceptionally dangerous in Afghanistan, which has the second-highest rate of maternal mortality in the world.

Bottom left: When a woman of the Turkana tribe in Kenya gives birth, four goats are slaughtered to celebrate the occasion. The skin of the first is made into a pouch for carrying the baby on its mother's back. The small wooden balls on the back of the pouch are to ward off evil spirits, and the infant wears a bracelet of ostrich eggshell beads.

Bottom centre: A Dukha infant in Mongolia lies in a traditional crib suspended from the antlers of a roe deer.

Bottom right: A Nocte woman in Arunachal Pradesh, India, carries her grandchild strapped to her back. As in many other cultures, grandparents play an important role in child-rearing. The Noctes live in longhouses with their extended families, so babies and children are frequently attended by older relatives.

Above: Himba mothers in Namibia with their children. A child is cared for predominantly by its mother until the age of three, after which all members of the family are responsible for it. Children are encouraged to be as independent as possible.

Above: Yanomani Indians fishing in an Amazon tributary in Brazil. Children help their mothers with daily tasks and here they will collect fish that float to the surface of the river once a natural toxin is added to the water. The fish are carried in the baskets attached to the women's heads.

Courtship and Marriage **103**

The children of the !Kung of the Kalahari in southern Africa are never unattended – an adult maintains the constant vigilance needed to keep infants safe in an inhospitable desert environment. The !Kung share child-rearing and are calm, measured parents; they never discipline their children physically or harshly. In a Chinese extended family, a child is first socialized by its mother and grandmothers; later, boys are the responsibility of adult males and girls of adult females.

Ashanti villages in Ghana have brother-and-sister houses, where the sons and daughters of sisters live together. The husband and wife do not cohabit and the children divide their time between the households, raised by their aunts and uncles as much as by their parents. Among the Mossi of Burkina Faso, a woman goes back to her father's home and patrilineage after giving birth. She nurses her son or daughter in the company of her birth family and returns to her husband only when the

Research shows that San women burn up about the same amount of energy as elite athletes.

child has some independence, usually when it is about three years old. Even if the mother becomes pregnant immediately after returning to her husband, she must once again leave for her father's house after the baby is born. She takes the first child with her if it is a girl, but if it is a boy he remains with his father. The Mossi have a saying that expresses their belief that during the early years of childhood siblings should be brought up separately: "It is dangerous for two young brothers to urinate in the same hole."

Birth rates and fertility

The number of births in hunter-gatherer societies is relatively low. For example, the San tribes of southern Africa have children at a later age than people in farming communities, they generally have fewer, and the intervals between them are longer. Research shows that San women burn up about the same amount of energy as elite athletes; they walk many miles each day, often carrying heavy loads of children, food, or water. Their diet is seasonal, and their calorie intake is often low. This way of life is thought to be the reason for their generally low levels of fertility.

The length of time for which a San child is breast-fed may also play a part in preventing subsequent pregnancies – !Kung women in the Kalahari Desert average more than 3½ years between giving birth. The child is fed frequently throughout the day and night – its mother sleeps next to it – until it is about four years old. It has been suggested that as this uses a large amount of the woman's energy, her weight is relatively low and she is therefore less likely to get pregnant. Breast-feeding in sedentary, farming societies, where calorie intake is far higher, is not as effective a contraceptive as it is for hunter-gatherers.

In hunter-gatherer tribes around the world, although girls are often sexually active from a young age, and generally begin to menstruate in their mid-teens, they usually first become pregnant in their late teens; among the !Kung, the average age at which a woman first gives birth is 19 years. One theory put forward to explain this is that, for the first few years of menstruation, the girls do not ovulate regularly, a biological phenomenon that has also been recorded in girls in farming and industrialized societies. Generally, it takes a while for periods to become regular, and to be accompanied by ovulation every month. This means that a girl seems physically mature, but is unlikely to conceive until she is older, giving her time to practise adult behaviour before pregnancy.

Family planning

The environment in which hunter-gatherers live, and their low-calorie intake, controls their fertility to some extent. However, these natural barriers to conception are removed for tribespeople who live in farming communities where they expend less energy, and have a more consistent intake of calories.

In many tribes, the tried and tested methods of premature withdrawal and the rhythm method are used with varying levels of success, just as they are in other societies. Herbal contraceptive methods are also varied and effective. Incidentally, one of the ingredients used in the synthesis of modern contraceptive pills is diosgenin, a substance very similar to human progesterone, which is extracted from wild yams in Mexico and Guatemala. Similarly, the *Dioscorea* vine, which originated in China and has spread across North America, is widely used to manufacture a substitute for progesterone. Historically, extract of rue, which works like the "morning after" pill by preventing the zygote from attaching to the endometrial wall of the uterus, has been used across Europe.

Infanticide

Infanticide has been recorded in many tribal societies as a method of avoiding unwanted children. It is said to be practised by 20 of Brazil's near 200 tribes and infants are normally buried alive. Although the National Congress of Brazil has moved to criminalize it, this has been opposed by many people who defend the rights of indigenous tribes. Most Brazilian Indians do not consider infanticide murder. They see it as the kindest option for a sickly child who is unlikely to survive; for isolated tribal communities in the rainforest, illness combined with lack of resources often results in death. Amazonian tribes do not consider an infant to be a person until it has been ritually received by the community, so for them infanticide is morally equivalent to abortion in Western societies.

Among the !Kung of the Kalahari Desert, a woman gives birth in the bush, alone or with her mother. If she decides not to keep the baby, it probably never breathes as it is smothered as soon as it is born. This is not considered a sin; rather, it is a distressing necessity. The desert does not provide the tribe with much food, and children under seven are usually carried by adults for protection. In these circumstances it is not always possible to support an extra child.

When a marriage ends

Some tribes do not permit divorce. Among Hindu tribal peoples of north India, a high-caste wife was expected to merge her identity with her husband's to the extent that they could never be parted. The final proof of her devotion was to throw herself on the funeral pyre when her husband died and be consumed by its flames, alongside his body.

The status of widows in Hindu society perhaps partly explains why women accepted this premature and painful end. After her husband's death, a woman in a traditional family is expected to stay in his home and shave her head. She is considered bad luck, is excluded from rituals, and is forbidden to wear shoes. Although India's statute law authorized the remarriage of widows in 1885, this remains the exception rather than the norm, even for young women, though a widower is expected to remarry.

For the Inuit of the Alaskan Arctic, divorce simply means that a husband and wife no longer live with each other. In many precontact cultures, marriage has been regarded as an impermanent union – which means divorce is not a necessary concept. Customs differ among the Native American tribes of California. A Hupa husband can easily divorce his wife. If she has been bought, he refunds the purchase money – but can claim only half of it if he keeps the children. Wintun men seldom expel their wives, but slink away from home leaving their families behind.

So, some cultures, like the Inuit and Hupa, allow marriages to end; others expect them to last for life. Either way, marriage is a declaration of a commitment between two people. In all its different forms around the globe, it gives an insight into the complex human capacity for companionship, desire, and social organization.

For the Inuit of the Alaskan Arctic, divorce simply means that a husband and wife no longer live with each other.

Opposite left: Widows in many cultures show their grief and altered status through clothing. This widow in Papua New Guinea is caked with dried white mud and draped with strings of white beads. Here, dressing in white fulfils the same symbolic role as the black worn by widows in Catholic villages in southern Europe.

Opposite right: This Komo Vosavi woman has come to Port Moresby, Papua New Guinea, to celebrate Independence Day. Despite the festivities, she has covered her face with a mixture of charcoal and pig fat to show that she is a grieving widow.

Opposite bottom: Mindima widows in Mount Hagen, Papua New Guinea, remove a string of beads each day while they mourn their husbands. Once the last string has been removed, a woman may wash the clay from her body and is able to remarry.

5 Music, Dance, Leisure

Since the beginning of our history, humans have never been just hunters, gatherers, and providers. We have also been singers, dancers, storytellers, and music-makers. Recreation is one of our earliest occupations – even our hominid predecessors are thought to have made music and art – and modern time-and-motion studies have shown that tribal people often have more time for leisure activities than those who live in the industrialized world. Work is often combined with entertainment, when a task is turned into an excuse for communal storytelling and joking.

The sounds of life

Music is essential to almost all tribes, and their musical instruments, from drums to didgeridoos, are as varied and unusual as the music they produce. In particular, percussion – playing music by striking an instrument such as a drum with sticks – is a universal form of music-making, and usually accompanies dancing, rituals, or magic. The trance during which the soul of a Tunguskan shaman in Russia travels to the spirit world is induced and guided by the beat of a drum. In Ghana, Ashanti sacrificial drums were connected with death both in their construction and in their purpose. In the past, the drumhead – the part of a drum players strike with their hands or a stick – was made with human membrane

and decorated with the skulls of the dead, to accompany animal sacrifices made for the good of the tribe.

The Kaluli of Papua New Guinea, a tribe of mountain-dwelling horticulturalists, also associate their drums, and how they are made, with death. Drumming is usually performed for four or five hours as a late afternoon prelude to an all-night ceremony of dancing. To make a drum, they first cut down a magnolia tree, section it, and hollow out its trunk. Next, they capture and kill a tibodai, a bird whose song – "*tibo-tibo-tibo*" – is thought to be like the wail of a dead child's spirit. The drumhead is made from the skin of the yobo lizard, but the tibodai's feathers, throat, and tongue are also used ritually in the manufacture of the instrument to connect it with the spirit world. As the beats of many drums blend during the performance, the sound transforms from "*tibo-tibo-tibo*" to "*dowo-dowo-dowo*", the Kaluli word for father. This is interpreted as the voices of dead children of the past calling for their fathers; the ceremony seems designed to encourage the participants to release pent-up emotions.

The physical and magical construction of a drum is also vital to the Khakass, a Turkish-speaking people of south central Russia. A shaman enters a trance during which he receives special instructions from spirit guides – known as the masters of the holy mountain – which he passes on to specific drum-makers in his tribe. The instrument is made of willow wood and animal skin, and decorated with carvings of snakes and lizards, frogs and toads, bears, and reindeer. The first time the drum is played, the drummer is responsible for awakening its spirit. When it can no longer be used, the shaman's power disappears; it is said that he sometimes dies at the time the drum ceases to function.

Previous page: Painted and decorated Yari-Yari clan dancers at a sing-sing – a gathering of tribes or villages – in Tufi, Papua New Guinea. The aim of a sing-sing is to peacefully share traditional culture, dance, and music.

Opposite: A member of the Kaluli tribe of Papua New Guinea wears an ornate feather headdress for a sing-sing.

Right: Himba women in remote north-west Namibia – their bodies decorated with a mixture of red ochre, butterfat, and herbs – perform the *otjiunda* dance. They stamp their feet, clap, and chant while one of the group dances in the centre of the circle.

Global soundtrack

Some instruments are used the world over, and seem to have originated independently of each other. From Australia to Africa, the bullroarer is used to create a shrill sound like that made by a high wind. It is a flat, elongated piece of wood or bone, which is swung around the head on a piece of string. In South American and Australian aboriginal tribes, the bullroarer is played during male initiation rites – and is kept a secret from women. An image of the instrument, dating back to 4500 BC, has been found on the wall of a shrine in Catal Huyuk in southern Turkey, the oldest town so far discovered.

> From Australia to Africa, the bullroarer is used to create a shrill sound like that made by a high wind.

The Jew's harp

Like the bullroarer, the Jew's harp is found all over the world. It probably originated in central Asia, where women still play it to accompany traditional dances, and shamans use it to call on the spirits; it also has a role in wooing and courting. The oldest surviving examples were discovered in Japan and date back a thousand years. Despite its name, it is a small mouth instrument with a central tongue that is strummed with the thumb to create a reverberating sound when the player breathes against it. The reason why it is called a Jew's harp is unknown – no connection with Judaism has been established – but it is speculated that Jewish pedlars sold the instruments on the streets of London in the 16th century or that the name is a corruption of the old English word "gewgaw" – a gaudy plaything.

Left: A young Russian girl plays the national Altaic instrument, the *komus*, or Jew's harp.

Right: A man plays a Jew's harp in Sumba, eastern Indonesia.

The Tuvans of Russia believe the invention of the Jew's harp was inspired when hunters were puzzled to see bears stopping and listening to a tree that had been struck by lightning. Once the bears had gone, they saw that a fine splinter of wood was vibrating in the wind, amplified by the resonance of the tree trunk and creating a sound similar to that made by the Jew's harp. The instrument has a new lease of life in the 21st century: a multitongued version, the Chinese *kou xiang*, is finding fame on YouTube as an "acoustical synthesizer" perfect for New Age trance dancing.

Flutes and pipes

Pan flutes or panpipes are ancient instruments, the most famous of which are the Antara and Zampona pipes of the Andes that usually consist of 10 or more closed pipes of gradually increasing length. The player blows horizontally across their open ends, and although each pipe gives out only one note, multiple notes and harmonies are created when two or more are blown together; the classical modern flute is a descendant of this instrument. The pan flute has travelled the world – in Romania it is called *nai*, from the Romanian word for the Middle Eastern reed flute – and its sound has been resurgent in popular music in recent decades.

The nose flute is played by exhaling through the nose rather than blowing through the mouth. Versions are found in Africa, China, and India, but it is most often associated with Polynesia and the Pacific Rim. In Hawaii, it is known as *ohe hano ihu* – bamboo, breath, nose – and is traditionally used to serenade a woman and win her affection. Hawaiians believe that the nose is less polluting than the mouth (through which food, words, and vomit pass) and that the sound produced by a nose flute is therefore purer than that made with a mouth instrument. In the

Left: A panpiper performs at the first annual Melanesian Arts Festival in Honiara, the Solomon Islands.

Right: Quechua Indians play flutes at a village festival in Ayata in the Andes of Bolivia.

Philippines, the bamboo *kalaleng* of the Bontok people is long and narrow. Even when it is played by exhaling air from a single nostril, it is possible to produce a scale ranging over two octaves, using finger stops along the side of the pipe.

Millennia of music

Musical instruments have not only travelled huge distances but have been passed down over millennia. Rock art provides the earliest evidence of music-making in an image dating from 15,000 BC, when Europe and America were icy plains roamed by sabre-toothed mammals and small groups of hunter-gatherers. In the limestone cave of Les Trois Frères in south-west France, a prehistoric artist has depicted a man wearing an animal skin and drawing a percussion stick over an instrument. He is known as "the sorcerer", and the instrument seems to be a close relative of the Jew's harp: the mouth bow. This is basically a hunting bow that is held close to the mouth and can be plucked with the fingers as well as being played with a stick. It was probably invented by a hunter who used his bow in this way to flush out his prey.

The rock art of the Drakensberg range in southern Africa shows the musical links between the hunter-gatherers who lived in the mountains thousands of years ago and the Basotho people of the highland kingdom of Lesotho (a landlocked country entirely surrounded by the Republic of South Africa). The Basotho musical bow is thought to be derived from the /*khoa* – a hunting bow used by the nomadic San, who were probably the earliest settlers in the area. The /*khoa* was a mouth-resonated bow that was played very simply, without using the fingers to change the length of the resonating portion of the string. About half a dozen San rock paintings showing men playing the /*khoa* have been found in the Drakensberg range.

Opposite: A man from the Kenyah tribe of the Dyaks plays the *silingut*, or nose flute, in Sarawak, Borneo.

Left: A petroglyph in the Galisteo basin, New Mexico, depicts a hump-backed flute player known as Kokopelli, a fertility deity. It is thought that Native American tribes in the south-western United States have venerated him for over 1000 years.

Percussion and places

The sound made by many percussion instruments is intimately linked with the people and landscape that made and inspired them. The *tar* is a frame drum – its drumhead is wider than the depth of the drum – used by many indigenous groups throughout the Middle East; the Bedouin are an example. The drumhead itself is made from a goat skin that is heated on a fire until it contracts to the required tension. The drummer plays the skin delicately with his fingertips to produce the sound of dry, whispering air, reminiscent of desert winds. The San hunter-gatherers of the Kalahari Desert in southern Africa fill springbok ears with pebbles, and wear them around their ankles to produce a rhythmic sound as they dance by firelight. Also in southern Africa, the Xhosa stretch a dried ox skin between poles driven into the ground. Drumming on this creates a resonant sound that reverberates around their *rondavels* (traditional round huts) until the whole village seems to be alive with music.

This page: The dry, delicate tones of a Berber frame drum (above), played here in the Atlas Mountains, creates a very different sound to the rattling percussion of anklets used by the Kalahari San as they dance (left and below). In both cases local materials are used to make a sound that becomes part of the landscape in which it is created.

Didgeridoos and taboos

Like the /khoa, the didgeridoo of the indigenous tribes of northern Australia has a long history. A rock art image dated to around 1500 years ago shows a musician playing the instrument, accompanied by two singers. To make a didgeridoo, a eucalyptus branch (the longer the branch, the deeper the eventual musical pitch) is buried near a termite mound. Over time, the termites eat the soft inner wood, leaving only a resinous outer tube that is finished by hand. A ring of resin is applied around the mouthpiece and is painted with animals that are said to have the ability to move from one environment to another – an example is the frog, whose habitat is both water and land. This may be an attempt to enhance the didgeridoo's ability to transport the listener to the spirit world.

The didgeridoo is traditionally played only by men. Women are not supposed even to touch it, and some aboriginal peoples believe that girls who break the taboo will be infertile. When HarperCollins Australia published *The Daring Book for Girls*, there was an outcry because it included a chapter on playing the didgeridoo. In later editions this was replaced with surfing tips and the rules of netball, and the publishers issued a public apology.

Below: Men of the Pitjantjatjara and Walbiri clans in central Australia wear traditional body paint and play the didgeridoo.

Praise and performance

Music is a common feature of rituals such as initiation rites. In Lesotho, Basotho boys mark their passage to manhood by performing songs of praise poetry, known as *lengae*. In the past, these expressed the importance of cattle, warriors, and allegiance to their chief. In *An Introduction to the Music of the Basotho*, Robin E Wells quotes a 20th-century version sung at an initiation ceremony in the highlands, which praises modern technology:

> *It's a Toyota, men*
> *It is white, the tyres are black.*
> *There it disappears into the village.*

Traditionally, the Basotho sing when they are working: men when they are threshing sorghum or stretching a cow hide; women when they are grinding corn with the stump of a *knobkerrie* (a club with a heavy, rounded knob at one end). The music gives the workers pace and entertainment while they perform their tasks. Typically, the song has a syncopated beat, with the vocal falling between the worker's physical movements. This is similar to the early blues of America, elements of which are derived from African work songs.

Above: A Kuba men's dance photographed in 1950. The Kuba lived in territory that became the Belgian Congo, later Zaire, and then the Democratic Republic of the Congo. The once powerful Kuba kingdom fractured and dispersed during colonialism, and the Kuba now no longer exist as a distinct group, though Kuba sculptures fetch large sums on the black market.

Above: Muria tribespeople perform their famous bison-horn dance in the village of Nayanar in India's Bastar district. The dance is accompanied by percussion from the *dhol* drums played by the men and the *jhumka lathi* (iron sticks with bells) pounded by the women.

Music, Dance, Leisure   119

Songs for daily life

The Baka pygmies of central Africa (in particular, the Congo, the Central African Republic, and Cameroon) are known for their music-making. It is characterized by its use of vocal counterpoint, a complicated choral style where different voices combine to create complex harmonies. The singers often improvise together for hours. This beautiful sound permeates daily life. There are songs for entertainment, as well as for hunting, fishing, birth, death, and marriage. The full range of Baka music includes water drumming: an empty vessel is turned upside down and plunged rhythmically into water to make a pleasing sound as the air inside it is compressed by the incoming water. The Baka also use the bow harp, harp zither, and string bow.

Right: A Baka man from Cameroon dances to music. Baka singing styles are vocally elegant and technically complex, using multiple melodic lines that occur simultaneously – a technique also used in the baroque music of 16th-century Europe.

Opposite: Naro San in the Kalahari Desert perform a dance as the sun sets. The San homelands of southern Africa are a likely cradle for the evolution of modern humans, and the rock art of the region indicates that dance and music have been essential to San culture for millennia.

There are times when musical performances are competitive. Because of the scarcity of work and resources in their tribal villages, Basotho men frequently migrate to South Africa where they are employed in the country's gold mines. Here they perform in exhibitions of music and dance, competing with teams from the Zulu, Xhosa, and Swazi areas. Under the divisive system of apartheid, this gave men a rare chance to demonstrate their identity as a powerful group. Migrants also compete individually. One Basotho song tells the story of a tragic mining accident:

> *Mount Machai fell down, people,*
> *It's where a hundred people died;*
> *It's I who remained, a cannibal man.*
> *I remained, alone among that tribe [of corpses]*
> *I was pulling corpses from under rocks.*

As well as describing the dangers of working in a mine, this is a metaphor for winning the competition. The man compares his beaten opponents to the men killed in the accident. This is comparable to an Inuit song competition where singers will settle disputes in front of an audience, competing peaceably for the loudest applause.

Music's partner

Dance requires music and, like music, it is recorded in every known culture. Tribal dances can be celebratory, communal, and festive. In the Kalahari, !Kung from different areas meet to take part in communal dances that enable them to communicate and establish relationships with far-flung neighbours.

Ubakala dance-plays in Nigeria are performed at times of change, and can express the tribe's response to death, and sometimes to community problems such as conflict with outsiders. Dance can also be aggressive: the Maori people of New Zealand have a distinctive musical culture, and fuse song and dance to create the *haka*, performed by the All Blacks, the country's rugby team, before an international match. Originally a war dance, the *haka* combines menacing facial expressions (including sticking out the tongue as far as it will go), violent body slapping, and fierce shouts.

The Ghost Dance: a political statement

Tribal dances can be political. An example is the Ghost Dance of the Native American tribes of the United States, which expressed their desperation in the face of unstoppable change. It originated in about 1888 after devastating epidemics of typhoid and other diseases had ravaged indigenous populations. A shaman of the Paiute tribe in Nevada announced he had experienced a vision that the recently deceased would return to the land of the living, white settlers would be driven away and the traditional tribal way of life would be restored. He begged his community to perform circle dances to bring about his revelation. Versions had already existed throughout much of the north-western United States and his message spread rapidly.

> The Ghost Dance of the Native American tribes of the United States expressed their desperation in the face of unstoppable change.

In 1890, in an attempt to accommodate white farmers from the east, the government divided the huge Sioux reservation of South Dakota into smaller areas, and tried to force the tribe to abandon many of its traditional ways of life. In an environment that was hostile to cultivation, the Sioux's agricultural efforts produced very little food and, as bison had been nearly eliminated from the plains a few years earlier because of overhunting, they began to starve. Performances of the Ghost Dance increased in frequency and intensity, and the authorities brought in thousands of troops in an attempt to keep control of the area. In 1890, Sitting Bull, the Sioux chief, was arrested for allowing the dances to continue. A Sioux who witnessed his arrest fired at a soldier, which prompted an immediate conflict that led to deaths on both sides, including that of Sitting Bull. This led to the Battle of Wounded Knee, during which more than 150 Sioux, mostly women and children, were massacred by US troops.

Storytelling: a powerful tradition

Stories are told in villages in central Africa, in outrigger boats on the Pacific, in the Australasian bush, by the light of a seal-oil lamp in igloos, and around the fire in clearings in the Amazon rainforest. Some can be told by anyone, but in many tribes telling stories is a job for professionals. In southern Africa, for example, Zulu "praise poets" eulogize an honoured noble with tales of his attributes and achievements. They perform at state functions and other life events such as funerals. In West Africa, the storyteller is known as a *griot*.

This tribal figure became famous in the industrialized world through Alex Haley's novel *Roots*, which tells how, in the 18th century, Haley's ancestor Kunta Kinte was brought from the Gambia to work as a slave in Maryland. The modern family in America had their own *griot*, their grandmother, who told stories of her ancestry to her grandchildren. This inspired Haley to find out more about his African background. His research eventually led him to a Gambian village where one of the elders recited the local genealogies to him – and mentioned the name Kunta Kinte. When Haley asked him for more information, the elder returned to the present and worked his way back to the 18th century; he had learned the list

Below: A Qashqa'i man in a village near Bishapur, Iran, uses a bamboo flute to accompany the folk tales he tells in the form of songs.

Shadow puppets

Shadow puppets are found all over the world, from Greece and Turkey to Java, Bali, and China. It is said that they were invented by the nomadic Turkish tribes of the Eurasian steppes who used the sides of their tents for shadow shows. They are also said to have originated in China in 121 BC when the Han emperor Wu-Ti was so overcome with grief at the death of his favourite concubine that he ordered his court musician to summon back her spirit. The wily courtier invented shadow puppets to carry out his master's wishes. They became a popular form of entertainment in China's villages, and the repertoire of plays increased. Chinese puppets are made of animal skin, usually donkey, which is stretched and treated until it becomes translucent. It is then cut to shape and dyed to give different-coloured shadows when light shines through it. The puppets are surprisingly robust despite their fragile appearance.

of names by rote and could not disentangle them. Haley's version of what he learned from the elder appears in his novel and shows the compelling power of oral history. A well-researched academic essay that cast doubt on the veracity of the *griot*'s Kunta Kinte story has done nothing to stop it being repeated and passed on.

A poet of the north

Some tribal storytellers were famous beyond the areas where they lived. Orpingalik, a member of the Netsilik Inuit group of northern Canada, is an example. An oral poet, he first became known in the industrialized world in the early 1920s, when the Danish anthropologist and explorer Knud Ramussen interviewed him during an expedition to collect Inuit songs, poetry, and artefacts.

As well as being a great poet, Orpingalik was a renowned hunter and shaman, and a possessor of magic songs and spells. As a result of his command of the tribe's myths, he had leadership status and prestige within his community. His life was as dramatic as his stories, and the Netsilik ascribed some of the bad luck he suffered to his prowess with words. His son, Inugjag, died in his arms after a hunting trip. Both man and boy were sucked under a great ice floe and when Orpingalik regained consciousness he found he had been washed to the side of the river. He swam downstream in search of his son, and eventually found his body partially submerged. He took Inugjag from the water

and tried to call him to life, but although the boy began to breathe again he did so only momentarily. According to the tribe, the accident was a result of Orpingalik's battle with another shaman whom he had offended in poems rich with insult. The shaman had directed his magic against him, but as the man himself was too powerful to kill he took the life of his son instead. Orpingalik was also a murderer and an exile: he was outlawed for a number of years after killing a hunting companion in a fit of temper. His poems and songs tell of sorrow and anxiety as well as moments of fleeting joy.

Myths: the reasons why

Myths, the ancient and sacred stories of creation, are known and recounted by many members of a tribe, rather than by a single storyteller. An Inuit myth that explains how fish were created tells the story of Sedna, a beautiful girl who refuses suitor after suitor until a bird persuades her to marry him and takes her to his own land. Only when Sedna arrives in the land of the bird does she realize that being a bird is different to being a human. It distresses her greatly. All the children she gives birth to are also birds. One day, Sedna's father comes across the sea to rescue her. He kills her bird husband and takes his daughter and her bird children into his boat for the journey home. There is a huge and dreadful storm and the father decides he must make a sacrifice. He throws his beautiful daughter overboard, and when she clings to the boat with her fingers he cuts them off. They

Right: Shilluk people in Sudan gather in the shade of a tree for a storytelling performance. The Shilluk pass on mythology, legends, and even history by word of mouth. Stories are an important way of keeping alive the collective memory of a tribe.

fall into the ocean and swim away – they have become fish. Sedna sinks downwards into the water. She is now the goddess of the lower world.

The creation myth of the Zuni tribe of New Mexico describes how in the beginning there was only the creator Awanowilona. However, this being's innate knowledge and power enabled him to exist in person, and he became the sun. He rubbed his skin and formed two balls with his cuticles, which he cast upon the waters. One ball became the Earth Mother, the other the Sky Father, and together they gave rise to all life on Earth. But they began to repulse each other and separated. Now Sky Father guards the sky and its stars, and Earth Mother guards the earth and looks after its lands, clouds, and rain.

Supernatural stories

Stories that have similar themes, however improbable, are found throughout the world. Changelings appear in China, in Celtic and Anglo-Saxon folklore, and are told by North American tribes. The tales centre on the most vulnerable people in a society: babies and infants. Fairies or other spirits of the otherworld, who are constantly on the watch for unguarded children, seize one who is by itself and leave something else in its place: a fairy or spirit disguised as the missing child, or sometimes a block of enchanted wood, which is animated and resembles the boy or girl to trick the parents into believing the changeling is their son or daughter. The story has been interpreted as a warning to watch children carefully, and also as an explanation for the changes that can occur during childhood.

The story of the swan maidens appears in the Arabian *Thousand and One Nights* and is one of the Welsh legends recorded in the *Mabinogion* in the 12–13th centuries; there are also variants in Russian, Finnish, and Magyar. It tells how what appears to be a flock of swans is a group of beautiful maidens, sometimes sisters. A young man who has discovered their secret falls in love with one of them, usually the youngest, and seizes and marries her. But the maiden misses her own people and eventually leaves her husband, transforming herself into a swan to fly back to them. She often flies upwards, to the stars. The Arawaks of Guyana have a similar tale in which a vulture replaces the swan; in Inuit folklore, the maiden takes on the form of an Arctic sea bird.

One interpretation of this story is that the swans have come from the timeless land of the dead for some respite from the kingdom of darkness; ultimately, they must return there to be reunited with those whom they love. Other interpreters see it as a moral parable that warns young men against marrying reluctant brides.

Jokes and riddles

Pointing, laughing, and jeering convey universal messages that can be understood with no need for words. In some cultures the task of communicating these messages is given to a man whose job is to mock those around him.

Board games

Board games similar to chess, backgammon, or draughts, which use a chequered board and two sets of different-coloured pieces, are common to most tribes. There are variations in style and rules, depending on who plays the game and where they are playing it. The Turkic nomadic tribes' chess "board", for example, is a cloth that is wrapped around the pieces and put in a bag, so that it can be easily carried by traders and travellers.

Alkarhat is played in Saharan Africa and is similar to noughts and crosses. Players drop different-coloured pieces – orginally dark brown camel droppings and white date stones, but today dark and light pebbles – into holes in the sand. The winner is the player who surrounds his adversary's pieces with his own. It is played in a variety of forms across the region; the Tuareg use *alkarhat* for divination as well as entertainment. Variants of the game are *mancala* and *warri*, and often involve a board with small compartments into which seeds or pebbles are put. A similar game, *bao*, is played in East and central Africa.

An example is the *vidusaka*, or clown, in Indian plays who is akin to the Shakespearean fool. In Ireland, the *fili*, a learned academic figure with supernatural powers who was also a clairvoyant and poet, entertained with mockery and jokes. Among the Ju/'hoansi of the Kalahari Desert, specific family members are known as "joking kin" and are expected to maintain cordial and affectionate relationships between relatives. They show their intimacy with extensive joking that involves insults, mock threats, and ribald remarks.

Riddles are often used to entertain and educate. In Kandhamal and its adjoining districts in the state of Orissa in eastern India, the Kandhas tell them in the tribal group's Kui dialect. They are usually told by grandparents, and the answers are often everyday objects in a child's environment:

"It goes out empty stomach, but returns belly full."
Answer: A pot used to fetch water.

"It goes out belly full, returns empty stomach."
Answer: The bamboo basket used to carry cow dung to the fields.

Other riddles refer to a child's body. For example:

"Two little brothers so quarrelsome,
Beat each other till they sleep."
Answer: Eyelids.

Games and competitions

The competitive instinct is universal among societies and tribes across the world. It can be expressed intellectually, through pastimes such as board games; or physically, in duels, contests, or team games.

Opposite: A wooden board and pieces are used to play *alkarhat*. The game was originally played using holes in the sand and the pieces were dark camel droppings and light date stones.

Left: Masai men play *bao*. The game is a popular pastime in East and central Africa.

Lacrosse

Lacrosse originated in games played by Native Americans in the Plains and Woodland areas across the United States and Canada. The Cherokee called it "little war", and the Mohawk "the little brother of war". Today, the game is often known as "stickball".

Native American lacrosse was different to the European version. Games often involved hundreds, and sometimes as many as a thousand, players and took place on open plains between villages. They could last for days on end, though the usual play time was from sunrise to sunset, and goals could be as far as 24km (15 miles) apart. However, the basic concept was the same as it is in the European game: players use their sticks to get the ball to the goal. People were known to bet valuable trade goods on lacrosse matches.

The sticks were wooden canes with nets attached to them. The ball was made from a variety of materials: deerskin, rock, clay, or wood. Rules were decided the day before play. To start the game, the ball was tossed into the air and the two sides competed to catch it.

As well as being enjoyable, lacrosse toughened young warriors – shamans often coached the players in their tribe – and games were sometimes used to settle intertribal disputes. Men and women did not play together; the women played a different version of the game that used different sticks.

Above: Cherokee women and men gather before a game of lacrosse in an Indian reservation in North Carolina, 1888.

Land diving

The ritual *gkol* performed on Pentecost Island in the archipelago of Vanuatu in the south-west Pacific is the tribal predecessor of Western bungee-jumping – a sport that involves the participant falling from a height while he or she is connected to a fixed object by an elasticated cord attached to a harness or their ankles.

Legend has it that a man by the name of Tamalie had a quarrel with his wife. She ran away and climbed a banyan tree where she wrapped vines around her ankles. When Tamalie came up to her, she jumped from the tree and her husband, not knowing about the vines, followed her. He died, but his wife survived. The men of her village were impressed by her performance and began to practise jumps similar to hers. Eventually, this "land diving" developed into a ritual that was performed to increase the yam harvest, and became a way in which a Vanuata man could prove his manhood; the divers constructed tall platforms from which to launch themselves.

Left and far left: The land dive, the forerunner of the modern bungee-jump, is a fertility rite to celebrate the yam harvest on Pentecost Island in Vanuatu. Lianas attached to the ankles of the diver will snap taut and break his fall before he hits the ground.

The Matses, a tribe of about 2500 people in the remote Peruvian Amazon, entertain each other with competitions to see who can sneeze most vigorously and impressively. They use different types of snuff, some tobacco-based, and some made by mixing the leaves of the rare *nu-nu* tree mixed with the ash of bark. The snuff is a stimulant and taking it requires two people: a giver and a receiver. The giver puts a little powder in one end of a hollow wooden tube, and the receiver places the other end of the tube just inside his nostril. The giver then blows sharply down the tube, blowing the snuff into the receiver's nose. Experiencing this has been described as an explosion in the face that burns the nose and eyes, and blurs vision. Repeated snuff-taking leads to numbness and hallucinations.

Ear pulls and knuckle hops

The Inuit have long competed against fellow tribesmen in extended competitions that involve many different sports. The first World Eskimo Olympics was held in 1961, in Fairbanks in Alaska. This later expanded to include competitors from Canada as well as Alaska, and along with the Arctic Winter Games it showcases the games of the Arctic tribes.

These have traditionally been tests of pain, endurance, and skill. Some, like seal-skinning and fish-cutting contests, require the practical expertise necessary for survival in the tough Arctic environment. Others have the potential to cause grievous injuries. In 1982, the organizers of the Arctic Winter Games dropped two events, the ear pull and the knuckle hop, much to the dismay of the competitors. The ear pull involves two men linked by a thin strip of leather, each end of which is looped around one of their ears; the opponents pull away from each other until the leather is freed from the ear of one of them or one of the competitors surrenders in pain. Competing in the knuckle hop involves getting into a push-up position and hopping forward on knuckles and toes. Few men can stand the pain, and the average distance covered by those who can is 6m (20ft).

Another traditional game is *nalukatuk*, or blanket toss, which originated in Inuit whaling communities as part of the celebrations after a successful hunt; it is still a feature of whaling feasts, which are staged about once a year. The player crouches on a blanket, which is pulled taut by a group of helpers and then moved up and down so that he is tossed into the air. The person who is thrown the highest wins, but there are also marks for style.

As with the Inuits, leisure activities across the world reflect the environment in which a tribe or society lives. And whether they take the form of playing music, dancing, storytelling, or taking part in competitive games and sports, they are as basic to our lives as eating and drinking.

Above: The *nalukatuk*, or blanket toss, originated in Inuit hunting festivals. The blanket is traditionally made of tough animal skins, which can withstand the weight of the jumper, and functions in the same way as a trampoline.

The knuckle hop involves getting into a push-up position and hopping forward on knuckles and toes.

Across the world we organize ourselves into societies and tribes in order to create stable environments in which to live and bring up our children. For these communities to be successful, it is necessary for us to be able to communicate with each other, to have forms of government, to have laws that must be obeyed, and penalties for anyone who breaks them. Even warfare must have codes that are accepted, both within and outside a community, and we have evolved ways of indicating to an enemy that a conflict has run its course – and peace should prevail.

Communicating without words

More than 2700 languages are spoken in the world today, and our ability to speak means that we can communicate complicated and abstract ideas between individuals and groups. However, a spoken language is not the only means of human communication. In Australia, the *corroboree* (an anglicized version of *caribberie*) is a lengthy ceremonial meeting that facilitates long-distance communication between tribes; it provides aboriginal groups dispersed over a wide area with the opportunity to meet and exchange ideas and information. Dance, music, costume, and body paint are

used to enact mythological events. In this way complicated and detailed knowledge of tribal culture and the Dreaming – the hundreds of tales that form the mythology of aboriginal Australia (*see* page 154) – are passed on to the next generation. Everyone attending a *corroboree* is allowed to participate in some of the dances, but other dances are restricted and can be performed and watched only by certain people within the tribe; they illustrate special knowledge that only they should be privy to. For example, there are dances and music no woman should ever experience and, similarly, women perform some dances that should never be seen by men. Dance has become communication.

In Africa, languages such as that of the Yoruba tribe in Nigeria are tonal: the meaning of a word is conveyed as much by its pitch as by how it is spoken. Words can be conveyed by whistling, and it is possible to whistle an entire conversation. It is common to communicate over distances in this way; as two people come closer to each other, they may switch from whistled to spoken speech in mid-sentence. Similarly, the Yoruba, and also the Ashanti of Ghana and the Hausa of Niger, use hourglass-shaped "talking drums" that imitate the rhythms and intonations of spoken words by reproducing their pitch. These drums are one of the tools of the *griot* (*see* page 122), and are used at the beginning of a storytelling session to bring the community together. They are also used to communicate precise dialogue to the listeners.

The slit gong is used by peoples in the rainforests of Africa, such as the Bassa tribe of Cameroon and the Efik of Nigeria. It has a hollow chamber and a long, narrow slit, and is beaten to produce a rhythm of high and low notes. As the sound carries for about 6.5km (4 miles), the gong can be used to send messages between villages. In the past, missionaries and colonial officials were astonished to arrive in remote

Previous page:
A *corroboree* in Arnhem Land, Northern Territory, Australia. Recent research suggests that most aboriginal people practise Christianity in some form, but there is still widespread belief in the myths and teachings of the Dreaming. The *corroboree* celebrates this mythology and passes it on to the next generation.

Opposite: In northern Ghana, drums are carved from hardwood to make carefully tuned instruments. During the time of the slave trade, they were banned in West Africa to prevent slaves communicating over long distances in codes unknown to traders and masters. Despite this prohibition, drumming has remained an important element in West African music.

Right: On Ambrym Island, Vanuatu, a man beats on a large slit drum to send a message across the island. The sound of such drums carries for miles, and is most frequently used to call people to attend communal gatherings.

villages in the rainforest to find the inhabitants not only knew they were coming but also how many people were in their party – and even the purpose of their visit.

This type of aural semaphore is used in New Guinea, and was a means of communication for Native Americans in times of war: they played solos on snare drums, usually made with a gut snare stretched across the bottom of a hollow wooden shell, to broadcast their unit's success or failure. When Africans were transported to the Caribbean and America as a result of the slave trade, they took the drum language with them – and used it to send messages in a code unknown to their owners.

Law and government

Communication is not only about conveying ideas and simple instructions; it is also about establishing, and maintaining, how a society or community is organized – how it is governed. Debate must be turned into decisions, and in tribes, as in nations, these decisions may be taken democratically or by one person. Either way, they must be communicated to the entire community.

Among the tribes of the Melanesian islands in the western Pacific, men compete to gain a following and so take charge of an area. These "big men" are not elected formally, but a man who is acclaimed as leader is expected to represent the interests of his village in negotiations with neighbours and outsiders. Alternatively, there may be a centralized governing body, as there is in much of the industrialized West – authority is given to a few, and a judicial system imposes the laws they establish. In tribes with this type of hierarchy, such as the Swazi in southern Africa or the Ashanti of Ghana, there tend to be greater disparities of wealth and influence. Also in Africa, the Nuer of eastern Africa and the Tallensi of northern Ghana do not have centralized bodies but are organized through the authority of descent groups and kinship obligations. In these tribes there tend to be lesser divisions in rank or status.

> A man who is acclaimed as leader is expected to represent the interests of his village in negotiations with neighbours and outsiders.

Boys' villages

The Nyakyusa are a Bantu-speaking tribe in the Great Rift Valley at the north end of Lake Malawi in east central Africa. Rather than living with their extended families, their residence is determined by their age. When young boys reach the age of about 10, they build their own huts in an area away from their parents. They sleep in this new village and to eat they return to their parents' community, taking meals together in the house of a different mother each day. Other boys join them and their number grows to between 20 and 39. When the original members of the group reach the age of 16, membership is closed to new 10-year-olds, who must start their own village. The members of the initial group live together for the rest of their lives. Young men remain single for about 10 years and occasionally serve as warriors. Between the ages of 25 and 30 they marry pubescent girls who live with them in their village. Children live with their parents, but sons move out when they are 10 or 11, and the cycle continues.

Once in each generation a ceremony is held during which leadership of the community of age-villages is ritually handed over from a village that consists of older men to a more recently established one of younger men. The men of this village are now the headmen of the Nyakyusa group of age-villages, and the two most highly born take on the powers of the chief. The younger men will fight for their leaders if necessary. The retirees of the "older" village have ritual and advisory roles.

Absolute rulers

The Ashanti and Swazi, and the Ganda of Uganda, are tribes who live under the direct and absolute rule of a king, but there are established practices that try to prevent the abuse of power. The ruler may have to consult councillors before he can make a decision; his mother has the right to scold him in public; and relatives may rebuke him or even – if they have popular support – start an uprising against him.

> The absolute ruler's power can be manipulated to enable less high-ranking people to have political influence.

In other systems the absolute ruler's power can be manipulated to enable less high-ranking people to have political influence. The Cottica Djuka tribe, in Surinam in north-eastern South America, has a hierarchy that descends from the "granman", the head of the tribe, to a tier of heads of villages, who in turn control people in official positions in their villages, and policemen. Although the Cottica Djuka are legally under the control of the Surinam state, the authorities recognize the tribal hierarchy and uphold the

Smoke and fire signals

Smoke signals are a form of visual communication that, in open areas, can be used over long distances. Aboriginal people in Australia send them to tell people where they are. In China, soldiers on the Great Wall lit fires on watchtowers to create smoke and warn of an impending attack on the kingdom by neighbouring tribes, such as the Tujue during the Tang dynasty. On the plains of North America each tribe had its own system of sophisticated smoke signals to indicate danger or tell people to go to a safe area.

To make the signals a fire is lit in an open area, and fistfuls of branches or leaves are added to make a large amount of smoke. The fire is covered with a blanket, which is lifted and quickly replaced to send puffs of smoke into the air. A code of signals means the rhythm of the puffs, and the amount of smoke, can convey messages over a huge distance.

Above: Starting a fire in Queensland. Similarly to the North American plains, smoke has long been used to communicate over the wide open spaces of the Australian outback.

dignity of the granman and other tribal leaders. In villages on the periphery of the Cottica Djuka area, granman's name is invoked when there is no obvious solution to a problem. Just mentioning it generally allows a compromise: everyone feels they are in the right and the dispute can be allowed to die down. Village leaders can use his name when they punish miscreants – for example, by ordering them to sit in the burning sun for an hour. They can also promote their own aims and interests if they are able to convince people that they have granman's support.

Social rules

Social rules can be as effective as laws. In the Trobriand archipelago, south-east of New Guinea, generosity is regarded as paramount and there is a system of public gift exchange. Not to participate in this sharing of resources results in losing face – someone who is a generous gift-giver gains the respect of their fellows, and thus status. The rules that keep a society working are based on obligations, exchanges, and rights, and do not always need a formalized system of government in order to work.

Crime and punishment

There is no culture where everyone can do whatever they want. There are always behaviours that are expected and some that are forbidden. All over the world humans accept constraints and face consequences if they ignore them. Some systems of tribal justice seem relatively straightforward: in the Andaman Islands

Above left: The Ashanti people of Ghana are ruled by a king. Here, the late Otumfuo Opoku Ware II, the 15th king of the Ashanti and a qualified barrister, is dressed in a kente cloth and gold, as is customary for the Ashanti ruler.

Above right: Mutebi II is the king or kabaka of the Ganda people, Uganda. A Cambridge graduate, he became kabaka in 1969, but it was 1993 before he was recognized by the Ugandan government.

in the Bay of Bengal, if a man is aggrieved he can take whatever measures he deems appropriate – but must accept that he will face retribution if his action is deemed excessive by others. Among aboriginal peoples in Australia, legal power is distributed among older men and punishment is administered by councils of elders.

Punishment can also be meted out by courts. Those of the Barotse of south-west Zambia range from family and village courts to the royal court. Cases are passed up through the system as appropriate. In the royal court, the supplicants and litigants present their case before the king, councillors, stewards, clerks, and police. Each speaker calls witnesses and kinsmen to defend them or support their accusation. The councillors cross-examine them and present their judgement to the king, who rejects or accepts it.

In other communities cases are dealt with more directly by the public. In the smaller lineage-based villages of Lesotho in southern Africa, disputes and breaches of peace are brought before village headmen. The whole community must attend the hearing, which is held in the *khotla*, an open space in front of the huts, and so participate in the administration of justice.

Trobriand Islanders use a particularly lively system of justice, called *yakula*, to resolve conflicts within their communities: the two opposing parties, along with their friends and relatives, harangue each other and hurl recriminations. Sometimes this is all that is needed for a disagreement to reach resolution; and it generally succeeds in showing the opponents where the balance of public opinion lies. In the Sunda Islands in the Malay Archipelago, notorious liars are shamed by their communities. When word of a lie spreads, villagers heap twigs on the place where the untruth was told, and the pile grows until it cannot be ignored and everyone is talking about the liar.

In the Sunda Islands in the Malay Archipelago, notorious liars are shamed by their communities.

Below: In Waipa village in Papua New Guinea, tribespeople use a compensation system for offences. This man has killed his wife and, to pay for his crime, is offering pigs and money to the community from which she came; his final payment will be determined through negotiation.

137

Self-punishment

Suicide in tribal societies has been described as a form of self-punishment. In the Trobriand Islands, serious crimes, combined with public condemnation, often lead the offenders to kill themselves. In *Crime and Custom in Savage Society*, published in 1926, the Polish anthropologist Bronislaw Malinowski described how a 16-year-old boy had a liaison with his matrilineal cousin – a serious offence in the eyes of the community. No-one had criticized the couple in public until the girl's ex-boyfriend, spurred on by jealousy, began to insult his rival. Directly afterwards, the boy, dressed in his ornamental attire, climbed to the top of an 18m (60ft) palm and told his community he had been driven to take his own life. He wailed, then jumped and died instantly.

Other cases of islanders who committed suicide in the same way are noted in Malinowski's study. An example was a betrothed woman whose fidelity was publicly questioned. Like the boy, she dressed ceremonially, climbed to the top of a tree, wailed to alert the community, and then dived to her death. In both cases the offenders seemingly could not bear the punishment of public condemnation. In fact, the offence committed by the boy occurred frequently; many Trobriand youths bragged about having relationships with their matrilineal cousins, and the illicitness of the affairs contributed to their erotic lure. Yet when individuals were condemned by their community for their behaviour, they felt it was necessary to punish themselves publicly.

An eye for an eye

For many tribal peoples it is important that the punishment is seen to fit the crime. The Kapauku tribe of New Guinea has a council of elders who have traditionally punished offenders in a variety of ways, depending on what they have done. They could order an execution – usually death by poison arrow – which had to be carried out by a close male relative of the culprit, such as a brother, son, or father. This punishment might be given in cases of murder, sorcery, violation of taboo, incest, selfishness, or the instigation of war. A beating over the head and shoulders with a stick might be appropriate in lesser murder cases or where someone was refusing to pay debts.

For minor offences, the council might advise slapping the ears; for theft or adultery, they might recommend the destruction or confiscation of property. Breaches of the peace have usually been

> In the Yurok tribe, the price for the murder of a common man was 10 strings of seashells.

punished by reprimanding the accused publicly while they squat in shame before the entire village. Banishment is an option the council would consider and a criminal could volunteer for this to avoid a harsher punishment. The Yurok tribe of northern California had an extended compensation system. Killing a man of social standing led to a payment of 15 strings of seashells, along with some red obsidian, a headband made from a woodpecker scalp, and maybe a daughter. The price for the murder of a common man was 10 strings of seashells. If a man's illicit seduction of a woman resulted in her becoming pregnant, he had to pay five strings of seashells and 20 woodpecker scalps.

Among the Gringai tribe of New South Wales in Australia, an offender was made to stand in an open area, carrying only a spear. Men of the village then threw spears at him – the number depended on the scale of the offence. If he could defend himself, he was allowed to live; if he could not, his death was seen as a just punishment.

Opposite left and right: Batak men take the bones of the deceased for reburial. Batak is a collective name for the tribes of the North Sumatran highlands. Christianity has been widely embraced among the Batak, but such death rituals combine Christian and traditional tribal beliefs. Many cultures around the world practise secondary burial, where the body is temporarily buried, and once the flesh has rotted away the bones are dug up and reinterred in the ancestral tomb. Among the Trobriand Islanders, the way a body has decomposed gives information about the death or the character of the deceased.

Revenge killings

Killing or injuring the offender is often the punishment for homicide. If a murder is committed among the Tlingit of the Pacific Northwest coast of North America, clans must theoretically repay one death with another, and a man, usually a relative from the victim's clan, must fight a man from the murderer's clan. But to prevent a cycle of revenge breaking out between groups, a high-ranking chief steps between the combatants with a symbol of his clan's crest, which would be desecrated if there was fighting. The opposing tribesmen may be left grievously injured, but at least there will not be a fresh cycle of vengeance.

The Bageshu of Uganda have also traditionally killed in retaliation, but the compensation killing had to result in a death that was equivalent to the original murder. For example, if a man had killed another man's son, the boy's relatives might have waited until the murderer's son was the same age as the victim, and then killed him. Similarly, the Giriama of Kenya have traditionally believed that a murderer must be killed in exactly the same way as the original victim. For most Australian aboriginal tribes, codes of honour prescribed that a murder must be avenged, but that the murderer himself did not have to die; a member of his clan could be killed in his place.

Punishment beyond the grave

It is often thought that supernatural punishment will follow wrongdoing. For example, the Trobriand Islanders use magic to protect property. A man who lays claim to a distant plot of palms will attach leaves to their bark to show that he has used a curse to protect them from theft. A potential thief therefore knows he would face supernatural vengeance.

The Trobrianders also believe that aberrant behaviour will ultimately be punished and can even lead to the offender dying. Most deaths are thought to be the work of sorcery, and villagers may exhume someone to investigate why they were killed by

Left: In the South Waziristan tribal region of Pakistan, men wait for a jirga – an assembly of elders that takes decisions on justice and public order based on consensus – to pass judgement. On this occasion, the elders ordered the demolition of the house belonging to a tribesman who had opposed raising a militia.

Below: On 22 September 2009, residents of Duk Padiet village, in the oil-producing region of southern Sudan, stood guard against the neighbouring Lou Nuer tribe. Two days previously the Lou Nuer had raided the village, killing more than 100 people and burning churchgoers. The conflict is one of a surge of tribal killings in 2009 and reflects the instability of a region that is yet to emerge fully from two decades of civil war.

witchcraft. The grave is opened and the body is washed, anointed, and examined. If scratches are seen on a man's body, it means he has practised adultery or been too successful with women. If the body is swarming with lice or its legs are apart, it is suspected that the person died because they caused sexual jealousy. Red, black, and white colours on the skin suggest that the deceased had been too ambitious when he decorated his hut; large tumours that his taro gardens may have been ostentatious or perhaps that the dead man did not pay enough of their yield to the chief. Loose skin peeling off in folds means he had eaten too much pork during his lifetime. These and other beliefs about what an exhumed body will reveal help to curb antisocial behaviour.

Tribal warfare

It is a sad truth that humans the world over have felt the need to develop exceptional skills in the art of warfare. Human history has involved a huge amount of invasion and counterattack, raids, and rapine. Tribal wars occur for much the same reasons as international ones, though on a smaller scale. They may be triggered by the desire for land or resources: for example, the wars between Native American tribes during the colonial period of the 16–18th centuries were fought to obtain better hunting and trapping territories. Sometimes wars are fought to acquire valuable goods, or an individual may wage a war to gain leadership and a following. Revenge can also be a motive for warfare. Sometimes, perhaps most often in polygynous tribes, wars are fought to seize wives. Tribal warfare can be defensive as well as offensive, and the motive behind fighting is often to protect rights, property, or lives from invaders. Wars can be fought with neighbours or outsiders, and are often given religious or supernatural significance.

Warriors and women

In most tribes, everybody who is able to bear arms is expected to do so. In some, such as the Dinka of Sudan, a man is born into a warrior class. In others, such as the Masai of Kenya, warriors are young men who have gone through the initiation rituals that mark the end of boyhood but have not yet married. They live separately from the rest of their community, and are not allowed certain privileges, such as drinking beer. Once they marry they retire from warfare and focus on domestic governance. In yet other tribes, success in war is essential to becoming a man: Dyak boys of north Borneo reach manhood only when they have returned with the head of an enemy. Women are scarce on the front lines of tribal warfare, though there is often a female presence in war camps. In the Middle East, Bedouin women who travelled with military units were said to have the task of stimulating the officers by showing their breasts, unveiling themselves, and unbraiding their hair. Women of the Ojibwa tribe in North America cut off the genitals of the enemy dead after a battle. Females are often forbidden to touch weapons because it is believed this will make them less efficient.

> Women of the Ojibwa tribe in North America cut off the genitals of the enemy dead after a battle.

Zulu fighting techniques

Because of the smaller scale of most tribal wars, standing armies are rare in tribes. However, there have been exceptions. The Zulu, who were the dominant tribe in south-east Africa in the early 19th century, are an example. The Nguni tribes had migrated into southern Africa from the north-west since the 16th century, forming small, scattered, and split tribes who worked a cattle-raising economy; one of these groups became the Zulu, and others became tribes such as the Swazi, Themba, and Xhosa. By around 1800, the numbers of Nguni people had increased to such an extent that there was increased pressure on the land, meaning that within the tribes bigger

and bigger units were formed. Dingiswayo, the leader of the particularly large Zulu group, established a wide-ranging chiefdom by waging war against other tribes, and defeating and taking control of them. In 1816 he helped Shaka, the illegitimate son of a Zulu headman, to become the tribe's warrior chief.

Shaka invented a new fighting technique to conquer neighbouring tribes and territory: the use of a broad, stabbing spear rather than a javelin. He and his men discarded their sandals to gain speed and charged their opponents, using their shields to push away those of the enemy, whose left sides were exposed to the Zulus' blades. This led to high casualties on both sides, but Shaka's troops created a kingdom of more than 200,000sq km (80,000sq miles). To defend it from invasion, Shaka organized a 30,000-man standing army.

The Maori way of war

Before Europeans settled in New Zealand in the late 19th century, its population consisted of 100,000–300,000 Maori who were organized into about 40 tribes. There were wars both within and between tribes, during which people retreated from the open villages in which they usually lived to fortified areas, or *pa*. Battles were usually fought for revenge, but also for territory. Warring with other tribes has been described as a means by which Maori groups maintained solidarity and unity.

The core of a village's population was a group of kinsmen, known as the *hapu*, which had a hereditary leader; it was an effective fighting unit on its own, but sometimes combined with other *hapu* to form larger units.

The chief of a tribe was usually highborn and in war, as in peace, was a leader rather than simply a commander of men; when defending a *pa* or mounting an attack, he was expected to inspire his warriors through exemplary action. He was always at the

Above: In KwaZulu Natal, South Africa, two Zulus demonstrate combat training. In the 19th century, the Zulus won an enormous kingdom through violent conquests, but suffered bloody defeats during the European colonization of Africa.

Opposite: The most famous of the Maori *haka* is the dance that was traditionally performed before warfare – a version of which is now performed by New Zealand players before an international rugby match. Shouts, slaps, and facial contortions show the aggressive energy of the warriors.

apex of the wedge formation that was used to charge the enemy, and gave the starting signal for an ambush. If a chief was killed during a battle, his Maori warriors often fled.

Battles were frequently short and could be decided in minutes; victory was claimed as soon as the other side retreated. The Maori kept debtor and creditor statements of the battles, which accounted meticulously for every life taken on either side. This meant that revenge could be accurately plotted and, as a result, there are numerous examples of wars that lasted many years and even down the generations. Most enemies were killed on the spot, but occasionally men were killed later, or sometimes enslaved.

> **The Maori kept debtor and creditor statements of the battles, which accounted meticulously for every life taken on either side.**

According to European reports during the 18th and 19th centuries, men who had been captured were on occasion devoured at cannibal feasts. However, these reports were often written by missionaries, and could be exaggerated and biased. They say that the flesh of captives was eaten and, to insult the enemy, their bones were used to make flutes, fish hooks, or rings to bind the legs of captured parrots. Skulls are described as water carriers and there are accounts of the heads of enemy chiefs being preserved, impaled on sticks, and exposed to public vilification. In addition to flesh and bones, other war loot might include food, weapons, tools, and the preserved heads of the enemy's enemy.

Prisoners were secured with their hands tied behind their backs and ropes around their heads. According to missionary observations of the 19th century, Maori slaves could be killed at any time as human sacrifices or food for a feast, but while they were alive they were well fed, were allowed to speak freely, and were kindly treated and not overworked.

Jivaro headshrinkers

Jivaro is the old name for a group of culturally similar tribes that live in the Amazon region of eastern Ecuador and northern Peru, an area of heavy rainfall, lush rainforest, and some mountainous Andes foothills. The Achuar and Shuar are just two of these tribes, and in the 19th century they acquired a global reputation as ferocious warriors and head-hunters.

Jivaro warfare falls into two basic categories: raiding between tribes and feuding within tribes. In intertribal raids, for example the Shuars versus the Achuars, each tribe was led by a prominent great man and, in the case of the Shuar, involved collecting the heads of slain enemies in order to shrink them to make *tsantsa* trophies.

During a feud within a tribe, the households of a threatened village would move into the large, fortified house of its great man. This is usually on a hill or in a bend in a river, and is protected by a ring of poles made from the wood of the *chonta* palm.

On the night before a raid on such a house, a log drum summons the warriors in the raiding party. They drink manioc beer, and exchange war chants with the host elder, or *curaka*, who may drink *ayahuasca* (a hallucinogenic potion) to commune with spirits about the possible success of the raid. If the vision he has is favourable, the warriors reassemble at dawn. They and a supporting party of older men, women, and children travel by river or by foot into enemy territory. Each warrior takes a chonta-wood spear for battle and a blowgun for hunting; over the last hundred years he might also have a firearm. On arrival, a base camp is constructed.

To avoid being surprised by intruders, the enemy usually lays traps in the approach to the house. An example is a hole, 1.5m (5ft) deep that contains three pointed sticks; a raider who falls into it is trapped or impaled inside this "hole of death". If the raiders successfully negotiate or avoid such obstacles and enter the house, the preferred method for killing is to throw or thrust a long spear into the enemy's neck, as this prevents the victim crying out for assistance and may help the beheading that will follow. No-one is spared: women, children, and even animals may be killed, though they are sometimes captured instead. Heads may be taken from all the men who have been defending the house. However, when the enemy groups are closely related, relatives do not take each other's heads.

Western surgeons who studied the exact procedure for decapitation found that the head is taken from the victim by incising a broad, deep, V-shaped cut in the front of the neck, from immediately above to the clavicles to approximately between the nipples. The skin is peeled back, and the viscera of the neck are transected as much as possible. A cut is then made as low in the back of the neck as possible, between two vertebrae. The process can take an experienced warrior only a few minutes, even if he uses the traditional chonta-wood spear – it has recently been greatly accelerated by the use of a metal knife. To make the head easy to carry, a loop of cloth or plant fibre is strung through the victim's mouth and out of his neck to serve as a handle; it may also be carried by its hair.

To shrink a head, the Jivaro would cut a vertical incision in the back of the head and draw the skin carefully off the skull in one piece. This would be boiled, sewn together, and then filled with hot sand and stones that would bake the head. Any excess flesh inside would be scraped off. At this point the head would be about the size of an orange, and would be painted black, with its lips highlighted in red. The hair would be left on the scalp because the Jivaro believe it contains the vital power of the avenging spirit. Three feasts would then be held to celebrate capturing the *tsantsas*. The last two feasts are hosted by members of the original raiding party, who must avoid certain foods beforehand and may not hunt alone. Both these practices are followed because the men are thought to be particularly vulnerable to attack by evil spirits during the period after killing. The final feast, held approximately one year after the raid, is the ultimate recognition of the raiders' accomplishment. The trophy has performed its function: the avenging spirit of the victim has imparted his power to the warriors who killed him. It will return to its home, and the head has lost its inherent value. Some sources state that depleted *tsantsas* are given to the household's children as toys.

Above: A Jivaro elder displays a *tsantsa* to two children – headshrinking is considered to have died out in the 1960s, but a black market in antique heads has continued and recent unverified reports suggest a gap in the market could drive a resurgence of the practice.

Far left: Warriors of the Jivaro region armed with blowguns and arrows. Today's warriors have new battles to fight as tribes such as the Achuar struggle to keep petroleum companies from extracting oil supplies from their rainforest home.

Left: This *tsantsa* is thought to have come from the Jivaro area in about 1910. The eyes and lips are sewn shut, and the hair is left long as it is thought to contain the power of the dead man's spirit.

Weapons of war

From the battle-axe to nuclear weapons, humans have come up with an increasingly imaginative and terrifying arsenal. Tribal weaponry is part of an endlessly inventive tool kit created in order to murder and maim. Some weapons are simple, everyday implements that take little modification to make them lethal; fighting with sticks is often used as a defensive combat technique in situations where fighters can only be lightly armed, and around the world it has been adapted for games as well as warfare. Fighting duels with sticks is a popular sport among the Nilotic Surma people of Ethiopia. Known as *donga*, it is regarded as the best way for a young man to woo a bride by displaying his masculine skills and physique; the participants in the contest are often nearly naked (*see* Chapter 4, Courtship and Marriage). The Nyangatom of the Nile fight duels stripped to the waist, and use a flexible whipping stick to mark their opponent's back with bloody stripes.

Prisoners of war

Tribes have special devices to ensure that prisoners, captured wives, or slaves are unable to escape. In the Gulf of Papua area of south-western New Guinea, a rattan loop attached to a spike was thrown around the neck of a prisoner; and several South American tribes used the *boleadora*: rocks were tied to the end of a long rope, or sometimes to three ropes attached at one end, and hurled through the air, in order to bruise, entangle, and even concuss an enemy attempting to escape.

"Green" armour

Tribes across the world have used bark for protection during battle. Tribal peoples in north-eastern New Guinea covered themselves with up to 12 capes made from bark cloth. In the Melanesian islands of the western Pacific and in Africa and South America, warriors wore corsets made from animal skins or bark under their clothes; and in Cameroon helmets were made of basketry. Carved wooden shields are common across eastern and southern Africa.

Small is deadly

Small weapons can be easily concealed when a surprise attack is planned. Rings and bracelets with spikes are found in Indonesia, Asia, and Africa. In the islands of the central and South Pacific, they were made with sharks' teeth and were dragged across an enemy's lower abdomen like a saw. The English explorer and navigator Captain James Cook brought one of these back from Hawaii. The tomahawks of North American tribes combined a blade, knife, and tobacco pipe in one weapon. The *tacouba* of the Saharan Tuareg, a long, straight sword with an ornate scabbard, was part of standard male dress.

Weapons have been adapted specifically for the environments in which they are used. The forest-dwelling Dyaks of Borneo attacked British expeditions with poisoned darts similar to those of tribes in the Amazonian rainforests of South America, but even these deadly weapons proved no match for firearms. While blowguns are useful in forests, slings are more practical for tribes who live in open country. Throwing-sticks, such as the Australian boomerang, are used both for hunting and as weapons, and throwing-knives have a wide area of usage that stretches from the Congo to North India.

Right: An Afghan boy in Nuristan has tucked his slingshot into a Soviet Army belt. This humble weapon can propel stones at high velocity and with deadly accuracy.

Far right: An aboriginal man in north Queensland, Australia, holds a boomerang – a highly effective hunting weapon that can also be used to injure or kill humans. It flies at high speed and can easily concuss an opponent, even when thrown from a distance.

Trophies of war

Taking part of an enemy's body as a trophy, or to trap their spirit, is common among many tribes. In eastern North America, Native Americans took either a small, circular piece of scalp from the skull of a slain or unconscious warrior, or a more extensive section that included the nose and ears, then dried it over smoke and mounted it on a wooden hoop. Some Plains Indians attached these trophies to their shirts, with the hair still intact. Philippine islanders used the jawbone from an enemy's skull as handles for Chinese bronze gongs.

Structures for peace

Given the endemic nature of warfare across the globe, it might be concluded that the arts of peace are not our strong point. However, some anthropological research has led to a more optimistic conclusion. The Inuit, for example, have never waged war among themselves, and their structures and environment are therefore worth a closer look. Their tribal groups are not strictly defined, and there are no class distinctions. Instead, the basic unit is the family – sometimes extended groups of kinsmen, who live in semipermanent houses, and sometimes single nomadic families. Occasionally, bachelors were adopted as servants. They were normally men without relatives, and were often disabled, ill, or poor. On average, the Inuit die young, and strong male hunters are needed to provide what is almost an exclusively meat and fish diet. So, for the tribe as a whole, living in a harsh Arctic environment, killing young men is risky. Intergroup aggression is released in competitions, such as singing matches and tough physical challenges (*see* page 129).

Above: Human skulls in Sarawak, Borneo. The Iban traditionally practised head-hunting and kept the skulls of their victims. Although these conferred status upon the victors, the main purpose in taking a head was to harness the strength of the victim's soul.

Bands of the Kalahari

Like the Inuit, the !Kung hunter-gatherers of the Kalahari Desert in southern Africa are a peaceable people. They live in bands that are permanently associated with a territory and are led by a headman; this position usually passes from father to son, but can pass from father to daughter. The bands usually consist of kinsmen who have grouped together out of necessity and for companionship. New ones can be formed if necessary; this is rare, but it can happen if a headman dies without an heir or there is friction within a band.

Stealing is rare in a sandy desert where a person's footprints are as well known as their face.

The !Kung faithfully follow the custom of sharing the meat that contributes only 20 per cent of their diet but most of their protein intake. The rule is that no-one ever eats it alone; it is distributed according to a complex system. Eighty per cent of !Kung food comes from plants, but these are very rarely found by chance. Instead, there are known places where tubers grow and groves of mangetti nut trees and fruit trees. Crucially, these are regarded as being owned by specific bands, each of which has many patches of edible vegetation that are interspersed with those belonging to other bands over a wide area. Rather than being shared like meat, plant food is kept within the family, but no family gathers more than their fair share. According to studies in the 1960s, no band had encroached on another's plant resources in living memory, and neither could anyone recall a single incident of a group fight.

Stealing is rare in a sandy desert where a person's footprints are as well known as their face. People are expected to avenge themselves if necessary, which can lead to the thief being killed, but the peace is generally kept – through meat sharing, gift-giving, ceremonial meetings, and a cultural expectation that all !Kung are treated like family.

Ending conflict

Conflict between individuals and groups is widespread among tribal peoples, as it is among nations. Yet, just as nations negotiate peace-keeping deals and truces, tribes have developed ways to bring fighting to an end and avoid further bloodshed.

The aboriginal peoples of Queensland, Australia, engaged in prearranged duels with many one-on-one combats taking place simultaneously. Opponents battered each other with clubs while attempting to shield themselves from their adversary, until the elder women of the tribe intervened and prayed for the warriors to let each other live. This enabled the men to cease hostilities without losing face. Because such combats were not allowed to develop into a general war, casualties were kept to a minimum and peace prevailed.

In the islands of the central and South Pacific, envoys of peace carried bundles of green branches to show that they came without malice and believed it was time to talk, much like the white flag of Western warfare. The chiefs of North American tribes, such as the Iroquois, literally buried their hatchets together in a symbolic declaration of peace, and sat together to smoke a pipe, from which we derive the saying "bury the hatchet". After the peace pipe had been smoked, tribes who had been fighting each other feasted together, and occasionally staged a mock battle. The Murngir of the Solomon Islands in the south-west Pacific also had sham battles at the end of conflicts, when the losing side threw genuine weapons at the victors, who were not allowed to respond.

On the islands in the West Pacific, *kava kava* is used to resolve conflict as well as to celebrate. It is a mildly tranquillizing drink made from the chewed or ground roots of the kava (*Piper methysticum*) plant combined with water, and people consume it primarily in order to relax without disrupting their mental clarity. Moderately potent, *kava kava* causes effects that last for about 2½ hours and are often compared to alcohol and Valium™: it relaxes the muscles and causes a state of happy, sociable wellbeing. Extract of the kava plant has been marketed in some parts of the Western world as a remedy for stress and anxiety. In the Pacific, *kava kava* has a political as well as a recreational function: opposing factions will drink it together and talk through solutions to their conflict.

Anarchists might be disappointed, but it seems that in every culture there is some form of social organization regulated by rules and customs. Whether we live in an empire, a kingdom, or, like the Nyakyusa, in an age-village, we develop a social system in which we make decisions as societies rather than simply as individuals. Tribes use a variety of ways to communicate these, from smoke signals and drums to the internet (*see* Resources, page 188). Sometimes, as with nation states, decisions are conveyed and expressed through violence and war. Yet whether they live on islands in the Pacific or in the Australian desert, tribal peoples have developed ways to negotiate and resolve conflict peacefully – a skill that is much needed in our increasingly populated world.

Opposite: In north-west Panay Island in the Philippines, the annual Ati-Atihan festival commemorates the ancient peace between the indigenous Ati tribes. Every January about 200,000 people converge on the town of Kalibo for the festivities, which culminate in a procession of dancers that writhes through the town like a giant rhythmic snake, demonstrating the unity of the people. This man is attending the festival with live snakes draped over his head.

Moderately potent, *kava kava* causes effects that last for about 2½ hours and are often compared to alcohol and Valium™.

How was the earth created? How did we get here? What happens when we die? Why do accidents happen? Why do we get ill? Can we cure ourselves? There are many places where we can try to find answers to these questions. We can study sacred texts, read science books, or gaze at paintings on the walls of ancient caves. Depending on the source, it is possible to conclude that our lives are controlled by God, bacteria, or beings from the spirit world. Across the world different tribes and societies have different belief systems, rituals, and rites that affect all aspects of their lives from birth to death – and each one also has a story that explains how the earth, and humans, were made.

How the world was made

Many creation myths are very similar: for example, the widespread story that the earth was created from dirt. The tale of the earth diver is widespread among the tribes of North America. It tells how the lone hero is floating alone on the primeval waters, accompanied only by animals. He asks one of them to dive to the bottom of the water and bring up some earth or sand. The animal tries, but fails, so the hero sends another, and another. Birds try, fish try, amphibians and mammals try, but they all fail. Eventually,

only one animal is left; it dives into the water and is gone for much longer than the others. At last it floats up to the surface half-dead, with sand in its claws. In many versions it is a beaver, but it is sometimes a crayfish, a muskrat, or a mink. The mud or sand it brings up is put on the surface of the water and expands magically to become the land that humans live on. This myth has similarities with the Old Testament story of how Noah sent forth the raven and then the dove to brave the waters of the Flood in order to find dry land.

In India, there are stories that tell how the earth was made from excrement. The myth of the Lanjhia Saora tribe in Orissa, on the Bay of Bengal, describes how the creature Bhimo defecated on the head of the god Rama, who moved so that the faeces were thrown into the air and splashed into the primordial waters; these dried up and the excrement formed land.

Freudian analysts have suggested that myths like these are due to male envy: men, envious of the ability of women to create life from their bodies, reimagine birth as defecation – something they can also achieve. The creation myth of the Chuckee people who inhabit the extreme north-east of Siberia comes closest to this theory. Raven's wife asks Raven to try and create the world, and when he is unable to do so she tells him she will create a companion for him. She sleeps, and during the night her belly rises effortlessly. Raven is frightened and cannot look. When she wakes, she opens her legs, gives birth to twins, and creates men. Raven flies above the waters, and excretes continually. Each piece of his dung falls on the waters and becomes land, and eventually the earth is created.

Previous page:
An Embera shaman in Panama prepares medicine over a fire in a hut made from palms. Throughout the rainforests of Central and South America traditional shamans provide medical and social help for the people in their communities.

Opposite: Dogon men in Mali read fox spores in the sand. The tracks cross a grid they have created so that they can use fox divination to foresee the future.

Right: In Haiti, a man balances a skull atop his head to mark Fet Gede, a voodoo celebration of the ancestors. Voodoo has been actively practised in Haiti since French colonial rule (1697–1804), and Fet Gede is a national holiday.

The Dreaming of Australia

The Dreaming of the aboriginal peoples of Australia is an account of how the universe was made, how life was organized through rules and morals, and why this was necessary. It contains hundreds of tales, some of which are concerned with the great marvels of the world: for example, how men first mistakenly used sorcery and now have to die from it; how hills, rivers, and waterholes were made; and how the sun, moon, and stars were set upon their courses. Another group of tales tells how men and animals became separated after their common past; how the kangaroo got its black nose and the porcupine its quills; how tribes, clans, and languages came into being; and how spirits were placed in waterholes and trees, and in the wind. The Dreaming is not entirely upbeat, however – people in its stories commit adultery, betray and kill each other, are greedy, and steal. And, unlike in many creation myths, there is no all-powerful being or deity; instead, there is power in the spirits, the people, the animals, and the land. There is no notion of heaven nor of hell.

Throughout the Melanesian islands in the south-west Pacific, people imbue objects with a spiritual power: *mana*.

Magical possessions

Many cultures believe that not just people but also animals and even things have a spirit or personality. The Iroquoian tribes of the north-eastern United States believe in *orenda*, the aura that surrounds people, and animals, birds, and objects. Just as the relics of a dead saint are sacred in the Roman Catholic Church, for the Iroquois artefacts have a mystic quality and are filled with the invisible power that permeates all things. Throughout the Melanesian islands in the south-west Pacific, people imbue objects with a spiritual power: *mana*. An amulet such as a stone necklace conveys this to the wearer, making him a better hunter, or a more productive gardener. The possessions of a powerful man contain his *mana* and can be a source of power for others; human remains, such as bones, are permeated with the spirit of the dead person.

Rituals and rites of passage

In its broadest sense, ritual refers to everything from how a guest is welcomed into a home to the solemnities of a High Mass, and plate-smashing during a wedding ceremony in Athens. What all these have in common is that they are either a way

Bottom left: This painting from central Australia shows the dark shapes of goannas – a type of monitor lizard – over a geometric design. Aboriginal paintings often show the bush animals that are central to the myths of the Dreaming.

Bottom right: Jazmin, an aboriginal boy in Yathalamarra, Arnhem Land, Australia, is prepared for his circumcision ceremony. He is covered with red ochre and an elder then paints him with an image representing part of his clan's mythology. Here it is *milmildjarrk*, a sacred waterhole (the circle in the centre of Jazmin's chest symbolizes the hole).

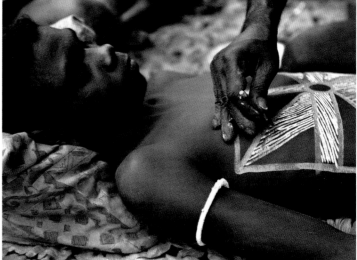

Museum collections

The significance that objects and human remains like bones has for tribal peoples means that the artefacts and skeletons displayed in Western museums are a source of contention and debate, particularly if the exhibits were obtained in morally dubious circumstances.

As a result of pressure by indigenous groups, many museums recognize that there were unfair exchanges in the colonial past, and are returning their collections. Swedish museums were the first on continental Europe to do this. In 2004, Sweden's Museum of Ethnography initiated the return of material to Kimberley, Australia, after Dr Claes Hallgren, a Swedish anthropologist, published *Two Travellers – Two Pictures of Australia*, which contained extracts from the diaries of Eric Mjoeberg, a zoologist who had collected aboriginal remains in 1910 and 1911. In the diaries, Mjoeberg described how he had obtained bodies without permission and smuggled them out of the country. This outraged many Swedes, and after negotiations with the Australian authorities tribesmen from Kimberley came to Sweden to take the bodies back for what turned out to be an emotional homecoming. Similarly, in 2008, four members of the Ngarrindjeri people of Australia collected six skulls and other remains of their ancestors from the National Museum of Scotland and Edinburgh University, and took them home.

In the United States, indigenous groups have campaigned for the repatriation of artefacts as vigorously as their Australian counterparts. In 1990, after years of debate, the Native American Graves Protection and Repatriation Act (NAGPRA) was passed; as a result, countless human remains and sacred objects have been returned to Native Americans who can prove cultural links to them.

Above: At a ceremony at Manchester University in July 2003, Major Sumner of the Ngarrindjeri of Australia holds a box containing the skulls of four aboriginal people. The skulls were returned to a sacred keeping place in the state of Victoria after being held in the United Kingdom for 100 years. Despite concerns about losing research materials, Manchester Museum (like the National Museum of Scotland in 2008) had agreed to the repatriation of the human remains in recognition of the unethical plundering and unequal exchanges that procured most of the tribal remains found in museum collections worldwide.

of mediating between men and gods, or they mark a social transition – often both. Anthropologists often divide rites of passage into three sections. First, there is a phase of separation; for example, when a pregnant woman or bride is removed from her usual environment. Next, there is a marginal phase, when the person lives in an unusual way for a specified period and receives special treatment from the community. Last, there is the phase of aggregation, during which the person is welcomed back into their community with their new status. All rites of passage are concerned with change, whether the rituals are related to birth, coming of age, marriage, or death. A birth or a wedding results in new kinship relations being formed. When a girl or young man is initiated into adulthood, those around them are expected to treat them differently. And when a person dies, relationships within a family are altered: a son becomes its head; a wife becomes a widow.

Death and burial

Death and burial rituals show not only the change that has happened for the deceased but also the changes that are happening for their family. They also serve to help individuals grieve and a tribe reaffirm its identity. Mourning rituals enable grief to be expressed, and are often spread over months and years in recognition that people need time to recover from the loss of a family member.

One of the early anthropologists who analyzed funerary rites was Godfrey Wilson, who worked with the Nyakyusa of Tanzania in the 1930s. Some members of the tribe were Christian, but many were not, and traditional funerals were the norm. Wilson noticed that they were far less solemn than their counterparts in

Above: Coffins hang on a cliff in Sagada in the northern Philippines. They are made from logs that Sagada elders hollow out and carve into coffins. The body of someone who dies is forced into its coffin and bones are broken in the process. Once a coffin is hung on a cliff, the dead person can join the ancestors of the Sagada. The custom of hanging, rather than burying, the dead is also practised in China and Indonesia.

Above: An opened coffin in Sagada shows the skull and long bones of a deceased adult, who by now will have joined his or her ancestors.

the industrialized world – it was customary to dance and flirt – and men and women had entirely different roles in the ceremony. The women's was to wail, which they started to do at the time of death, and continued doing until the end of the burial activities three or four days later. Until the burial, the women close to the deceased held the corpse in their arms and wailed intensely in a public display of grief. Women also wrapped their bellies in bark cloths in order to calm the trembling fear of death that made their stomachs queasy. Over the days, the focus of activity shifted to the men. Wearing cloth skirts and ankle bells, they held spears and leapt in wild war dances to honour the deceased by showing their strength. This emphasized male virility and strength, in contrast to the grief and fear shown by the women. There was a strong sexual component to the dancing, and men and women often left the dances to have sex, confronting death with an assertion of life. The roles of both men and women enabled them to participate in a cathartic release of emotion.

Many cultures provide money for the dead to cover the expense of their journey to the otherworld; examples are the Lolos of Mozambique, and the Moskito of Nicaragua. Ancient Greeks inserted a coin in the mouth of the corpse so that he could pay the boatman to ferry him across the Styx River to Hades. Death rituals often symbolize the strength of the deceased passing back to their family. In Bavaria, it was traditional to bake corpse cakes, *Leichen-nudeln*, for a funeral: the kneaded dough was placed on the dead body to rise, and when guests ate the cakes they also received some of the strength and virtues of the deceased.

The pollution of death

The dead body can be seen as polluting and dangerous to others, and this condition is often shared by close family members in the first stage of grief. They are regarded as ritually dangerous because they are between two states (for example, wifehood and widowhood, or son and head of family); they are also in contact with death, and can therefore bring bad luck. The Berawan of Borneo

Until the burial, the women close to the deceased held the corpse in their arms and wailed intensely in a public display of grief.

Left: A *nyubu*, an Apatani shaman in Hong, India, prepares to sacrifice a chick during a ritual for someone who has died recently. The Apatani believe that an untimely death is caused by evil spirits and that a *nyubu* is able to determine who is responsible for them by reading the folds in the liver of the deceased.

Right: Spirit money is burned as an offering to the dead in Wengshu monastery in Chengdu, China. Archaeology has shown that many cultures place money and valuable items in graves to accompany the deceased to the other world.

Opposite left: In Togo, a young girl dons a hat traditionally worn during initiation rites. It is made with cowrie shells, plant fibres, and gazelle horns.

Opposite right: Young Baka men in Cameroon emerge after a month-long initiation ceremony during which they are not allowed to speak. Anointed with palm oil, they walk in procession back to their village. This ceremony is becoming increasingly rare as the national government attempts to make the Baka, who are hunter-gatherers, assimilate into the culture of local farmers.

keep the corpse in a screened display cell for about 11 days. They believe that the spirit of the deceased remains nearby for this time, making it dangerous. Dressed in finery, the corpse is seated behind a screen of hanging mats and surrounded with valuables such as precious food and money to appease the spirit. The widow or widower remains next to the corpse, also in a deliberately tiny cell made of mats, and eats small portions of food. As someone who is emotionally and physically close to the death, he or she is thought to share its pollution, so is isolated from living people. The practice also protects the living spouse; the Berawan believe that the spirit of the dead person could be jealously vengeful and inflict death upon others, particularly those who were closest to them in life. Therefore, if the conditions of the widow or widower are cramped and uncomfortable, the spirit of the deceased is less likely to be jealous and cause them to die.

Initiation rites

Just as death rites show the changes to an individual, family, and community when someone dies, there are rituals to mark a person attaining adulthood. Initiation rites show the passage from childhood to maturity. For boys, they mark the start of manhood, and often involve a public display of the qualities males are expected to have as men of the tribe. Female initiation is often concurrent with marriage (*see* Secluding The Bride, page 100) as, for many cultures, this is the point at which a girl becomes a woman. In some tribes, visible symbols of adulthood are incorporated in initiation rituals, and can include circumcision, scarring, and lip plates.

Circumcision

Circumcision is common in male initiations, and is usually the essential peak of the ceremony. Among the Walbiri of central Australia, a male cannot enter his father's lodge, participate in religious ceremonies, or marry if he is uncircumcised. In most aboriginal tribes the rite is carried out when a boy is between the ages of 11 and 13. Only initiated men attend the cutting, which is the culmination of weeks of preparation. A tribesman seizes the initiate and places him face upwards with his feet towards a fire. Another man straddles him and presses his pubis bone against the boy's face to quiet his cries. A third man holds the shaft of the boy's penis, and one of the circumcisers stretches the foreskin several centimetres out while another cuts it off with a couple of deft slices. If a circumciser mutilates a boy, he faces serious punishment.

At around the age of 17, aboriginal men may undergo subincision, when the underside of the penis is cut to split the urethra. The practice is not compulsory, and is thought to be inspired by a lizard man from the Dreaming. The cut penis is said to resemble a vulva, and the bleeding is likened to menstruation. Men who have subjected themselves to this rite usually have to squat to urinate, in the manner of women. In some cases, the cut is later used for ritual blood-letting. In a subincision ceremony, the youth lies on the backs of two men and his penis is sliced to the accompaniment of loud chanting. As with circumcision, an incisor who makes a mistake is punished. Subincision is also practised in Papua New Guinea, the Polynesian islands in the South Pacific, and parts of the Amazon region.

Circumcision and separation

For boys of the Masai tribe of Kenya, the separation phase of their initiation ritual lasts for seven years, during which they are warriors and live apart from their community. First, though, they prepare for circumcision, which signifies the end of their childhood and their ability to face obstacles with courage and bravery. Other painful tests include teeth pulling, burning, tattooing, and ear piercing, but the most difficult one is the separation phase. The Masai divide themselves into age sets; boys born within a few years of each other are considered to be the same age. Circumcision takes place when most of the members of a set are teenagers. After this, boys are warriors, or *morani*. Initiates live in roaming groups, and sleep in the bush. They may have sexual relationships with unmarried girls, but are forbidden to drink alcohol. This phase tests their ability to bond with each other and survive in a difficult environment.

After seven years of living wild, groups of *morani* join together to march in from the bush and make their entrance to the *manyatta*, a village specially constructed for the *eunoto* ceremony that celebrates their initiation into elderhood – the phase of aggregation. They are joined by the tribal elders for a day and night. There is dancing, singing, and spectacular displays of jumping, and as night falls an ox is slaughtered and skinned. One of the *morani* drinks blood straight from the animal, and each initiate is given a small piece of raw meat, and a ring made from the ox skin that symbolizes the strength of their group. After the *eunoto*, the boys return to their villages as men. It is traditional for their mothers to shave off their long hair while they sit on the cow hide upon which they were circumcised all those years ago.

Above: Three Masai initiates with a small herd of livestock. Recently circumcised boys must learn independence and self-sufficiency during their period of isolation.

Top right: Girls are also circumcised in Masai culture, but they do not go through the same seven-year period of initiation. During their shorter time of relative isolation, they wear black with white beads, like this girl in Tanzania.

Bottom right: A Masai youth in the Kisongo section in northern Tanzania shows his recent circumcision and altered status through his black clothing and the white designs on his face.

Female circumcision, the partial or total cutting away of the external female genitalia, has been recorded in many countries. In its most extreme form, known as infibulation, it involves the removal of the clitoris and of the inner and outer labia, the raw edges of which are held together until they heal as scar tissue. The practice is usually interpreted as a means by which female sexuality and fertility can be controlled. It makes sex and childbirth extremely painful and difficult, and can lead to serious health problems caused by the flow of menstrual blood and urine being blocked. Among the Samburu of Kenya, girls are considered immature and promiscuous until they are circumcised. This generally occurs when a girl is about 15, just before she marries, in a ceremony in which she and her family's honour are fêted and celebrated. An unmarried girl in her late teens who has a younger brother may undergo circumcision before she has a marriage proposal; this is because a boy with an uncircumcised older sister may not be initiated into the warrior class.

The vision quest

During the marginal phase of change, an initiate is typically removed from his community, and may often be on his own. The vision quest of the Omaha tribe in Nebraska is a rite of passage where boys go out alone into the wilderness to fast and pray. Each boy is expected to obtain a guardian spirit during this time, and may be chosen by one of the many spirits of Omaha myth, who will come to him in a dream or vision. If a boy has a particular dream, he must dress and live as a woman while he is in the wilderness, even if he has no desire to do so, and must torture himself in order to receive his vision. This unusual behaviour, which would not usually be acceptable, is encouraged during initiation because the youth is not at this time part of society.

Variations on the vision quest are found in other North American tribes, and among the Inuit. Initiates are expected to acquire supernatural power through personal contact with the spirit world – this also applies to hunters, and shamans in search of a cure. Among the Crow in Montana, all success comes from receiving a vision and the person who is seeking one may try to obtain it by cutting off a finger joint, to arouse the pity of the supernatural world. Spirits can be seen or heard by the seeker. He may hear whispering in an unintelligible language, carried on the wind or in rushing water, or a celestial star may visit him. The vision may come in a recognizably human form, or spirits may appear as animals – anything from the majestic eagle to the rabbit.

Experiencing the light of Bwiti

In the Gabon rainforest, which is home to a number of isolated ethnic groups, both men and women may become members of a religious cult called Bwiti. It was started by the Mitsogos, but is now practised by other groups such as the Fang. To join the sect, initiates swear an oath – "*Na bwiti a besu*" ("By our bwiti") – then take enough of the root of the sacred plant iboga to receive visions of the sacred deities of Bwiti. All of these are represented in the temple where the initiation takes place. This temple can be a vast structure with a central, carved column that rests on the skulls and tibias of ancestors. The carved column represents the external sex organ

Top right: A young Pokot woman in Sigor, northern Kenya, wears a seclusion dress after being circumcised. The white paste that covers her face is made from milk and ash. Female circumcision is still common among the Pokot, and it is not rare for women to need hospitalization after the ritual, which can cause severe blood loss.

Centre right: A Fulani boy in Mali carries a wooden rattle signifying that he has recently

undergone circumcision. Some Fulani are circumcised in hospital, but other communities practise the ritual as it has traditionally been performed, and at the time of circumcision a sheep, goat or barren cow is slaughtered.

Bottom right: A Kenyan woman who has been circumcised wears brass hoops through her ears and large beaded collars around her neck to show her maturity.

of a man stretched on his back; its axis is pierced with a hole that represents the vagina. The walls of the temple may be hung with snake skins, brightly coloured trophies, and musical instruments.

Before taking the iboga, an initiate's face is covered with white powder to show that he or she is about to pass into the land of the dead. After taking the plant, they vomit and begin to see vibrantly coloured images. They then lose consciousness and fall into a deep sleep that lasts for days, lying on a mat laid out on the ground. During this time the initiate sees fantastic apparitions. An endless procession of masked, bony, lame, crippled, grimacing dead people files past. He or she then undergoes a thorough examination to determine whether they have seen Bwiti, how he appeared to them, and what he told them. If their answers are satisfactory, they are admitted to the sect. At the point of admission, a ritual solution made from *ibama ngadi*, the thunder plant, which burns like hot chilli, is poured into the initiate's eyes while he or she stares at the sun. The purpose is to show that now they have experienced the light of Bwiti they can look at the profane light of the sun without being blinded by its rays. As they grow older they will learn the secret doctrine of Bwiti.

Masters of the spirits

Many cultures, throughout history and across the world, have a role for the shaman: someone who is in touch with the spirit world. The word "shaman" comes from the Evenk peoples of Russia, and means "he who is excited". The Evenk believe that each person has two or three souls. If the first soul leaves the body, it leads to unconsciousness. If the second soul leaves for a prolonged time, the body dies. The third soul is thought to remain with the body until it

decomposes. A shaman can control the souls of himself and other people, and is a master of the spirits. Shaman is an umbrella term, which has replaced "witch doctor" – a phrase that unites the two stereotypical functions of the shaman: magical knowledge and the ability to heal.

Shamans act as mediators between worlds, communicating with the dead or with the consciousness of animals. In the industrialized world, quantum theorists propose a universe of many parallel worlds, and similarly for an Amazonian shaman there are an infinite number of worlds, each inhabited by different beings. Some of these spirits are protective and some are malignant. To become a master shaman, it is necessary not only to learn to negotiate different worlds but also to harness the powers of the beings that inhabit each realm.

The great dance

All the San hunter-gatherers of southern Africa, now and during the last century, have observed an important ritual called "the great dance". They meet in a camp and, using repetitive movement, music, and rhythm over hours, enter a trance-like state and they dance in a circle through the night. During the dance, the San feel themselves to be animated by a spiritual power that crackles through them like lightning, giving them the access to the power of animals like the eland – a large antelope. Dancing helps them to harness this energy – which the shamans can use for healing, rain-making, and hunting.

Paintings on exposed rock on the Drakensberg mountain range and in caves show the great dance, and San people have helped anthropologists to interpret them. There are images of groups of people dancing: bending forward

A sacred plant

Iboga is a small shrub (*Tabernanthe iboga*) with white, pink-spotted flowers and globular seeds that grows to a height of up to 1.5m (5ft). Its root tastes astringent and contains ibogaine, a powerful alkaloid that produces anaesthesia after a few minutes. In low doses, ibogaine reduces the need for sleep and makes it possible to resist hunger and fatigue. In high doses, it produces a hallucinatory experience that apparently takes an initiate into the Bwiti cult on an entirely believable journey through space and time, and can cause a state of lethargy that lasts four or five days. In massive doses, ibogaine may cause death by paralyzing the respiratory muscles. Intriguingly, animals are also interested in iboga – warthogs, porcupines, and gorillas all search for its roots.

Above left and right: Initiates prepare for acceptance into the Bwiti cult, Cameroon. Initiation

Decorative scars

Scarification is performed across Africa and involves cutting skin to form a pattern. In cicatrization, the cuts are irritated with plant juices, and charcoal or other pigments are sometimes rubbed into the wounds to emphasize them. When the cuts heal, they form raised scars, known as keloids, which can carry messages about identity and social status. Among the Yoruba of Nigeria, scarification indicates a person's lineage. Also in Nigeria, the Tiv find women with keloids highly attractive; they claim that these raised scars stay sensitive for many years, producing erotic sensations in both men and women when touched or stroked. For the Nuba of Sudan, scars show rites of passage.

The Nuba and other Sudanese tribes scar the breast, navel, and abdomen, though the practice is less common now than in the past. For some groups in Sudan this is part of the marriage rite. Before the wedding ceremony the bride undergoes some cicatrization on her arms, shoulders, and thighs. After she moves into her husband's house, she endures further cicatrization on her back, chest, and belly. In later life, a Nuba man may be cicatrized all over his body. The operation is gruelling and is in two stages: first, his arms, shoulders, and thighs are treated, then the rest of his body. A man marked like this is regarded as having enhanced his status (*see* The Body Beautiful, page 42).

Shulukh, or facial scars, are common in tribes such as the Nuba and the Azande of north-central Africa. Sometimes they are made to camouflage individuals from evil spirits: a child who is born just after its father's death, or after a string of deaths in the family, is given an unusual pattern of scars so that hovering spirits will not recognize it. When someone is grieving intensely after the death of a close relative, patterns are added to the usual scars, to hide the person from spirits or the evil eye.

Top left: Extensive facial scars show the facial contours of a Nuer woman in East Africa.

Top centre: In Ethiopia, horn-shaped scars in the centre of an Afar woman's forehead reveal that she comes from a cattle-owning family.

Top right: A Bobo woman in Burkina Faso is marked with geometric scars that have been carefully cut into the skin of her face.

Bottom: Masai warriors in Kenya compete in displays of endurance by placing hot charcoal on their thighs without flinching. These scars on a young man's leg demonstrate his ability to withstand pain.

Next page left: A woman from Ethiopia's Surma tribe with extensive scarification tattoos. The cicatrix are raised by rubbing ash into them immediately after the incisions have been made.

Next page right: This extensive scarification of a Dassanech man in Ethiopia shows that he has killed an enemy in battle.

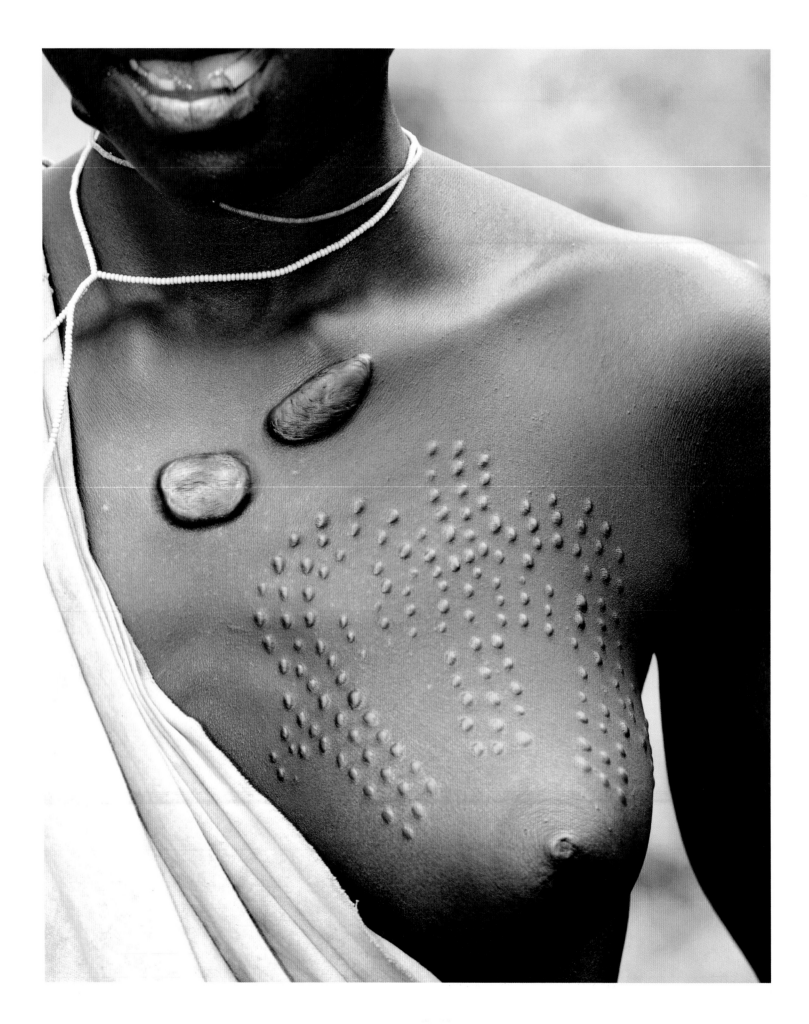

Above left: A Surma woman in Ethiopia wears a large wooden plate in her lower lip. The plate is considered a sign of feminine beauty.

Above right: At a young age, women remove the front teeth in their lower jaw, and pierce their bottom lip, which is stretched around a wooden plug. Over years they insert larger and larger plates; this one is made of clay.

Right: On occasion, the pressure on the skin of the lower lip means that it splits and the woman cannot wear the plate. This woman's lip is intact, but without the plate it hangs over her chin.

Lip plates

Women among the Mursi, Tirma, and Chai tribes of Ethiopia wear large pottery or wooden discs or "plates" in their lower lips. When a girl is 15 or 16, her lower lip is perforated and plugged with a wooden peg until the wound heals. She then decides how far she wishes to stretch her lip by inserting increasingly large plates over a period of months. Some girls continue until their lip can hold a plate with a diameter of more than 12cm (5in). For the Mursi, the plate is an expression of female adulthood and fertility, but its distinctiveness has made these women a prime attraction for photo-hungry tourists. Visitors to Ethiopia often seek pictures of the girl with the largest lip plate – and pay her with a handful of coins. It is possible that this is encouraging young women to stretch their lips further than they normally would, in order to earn more money.

wearing dance rattles, and holding animal tails and dancing sticks. Some of them are bleeding from the nose, which can happen when a San shaman enters trance. Some are depicted turning into eland, with heads and hooves. Animals pouring forth rain surround the dancers, as do other, mythical, creatures that are encountered in a trance. Sometimes lines connect the animals to the dancers. Patterns of dots and grids painted on the rock are similar to images reportedly experienced during a trance. The images are thought to be part of the harnessing and sharing of the spiritual power engendered by the dance. Generation after generation painted in the same place, with image after image overlaying each other.

> During the dance the San feel themselves to be animated by a spiritual power, which crackles through them like lightning.

One of the paintings shows a dying eland and a man who is thought to be a shaman going into trance. There are similarities between them: both man and animal have hooves, crossed legs, and animal ears. The San describe the shaman as "dying": he is leaving for the spirit world, and to facilitate his journey he takes on the power of the eland – its blood is often used as a pigment. Other paintings depict men "under water", a sensation that people feel during a trance.

Beliefs with a purpose

Magical rites sometimes have very practical purposes and effects. Hunting ceremonies can reinforce group bonds and promote individual endurance. Alternatively, when communities are threatened, a belief in external malevolent spirits can help them to unite against a source of fear – and may allow them to defend themselves against social upheaval. Religious movements such as cargo cults enable tribes to understand colonialism in the context of their beliefs, and mean their mythology is not undermined. Even puzzling phenomena such as spirit possession can be interpreted as ways for individuals to express difficulties and seek support.

Hunting magic

The Matses tribe in Peru uses the skin secretions of a poisonous frog in a hunting ceremony. After torturing it so that it releases its poison, they burn the skin on their shoulders and chest with a small brand from a fire, which quickly raises blisters that are scraped off the skin to expose the flesh below. The tribe's most experienced hunter mixes his saliva with the frog poison and smears it onto the wounds so that it enters the bloodstream – a form of rainforest hypodermic delivery. The effects are outwardly horrendous with copious vomiting and loss of control of the bowels. Some reports say the Matses see visions of game to be hunted, but others stress that the ritual is about the ordeal itself: if a man can survive the ceremony he is less likely to be reluctant to join the next hunting expedition.

Spirits for changing times

Pelacara – the name means face-peelers – are phenomena that turn up in different places around the Amazon and the Andes. When roads into the central Peruvian rainforest were constructed in the 1970s stories abounded about fearsome beings that patrolled them at night; they were said to kill people and bury them in order to build foundations for the roads. The Achuar of Peru have thought that oil prospectors in the Amazon, from the 1970s to the present, were pelacara who wished them ill. The Aymara of Bolivia believe in karikari, spirits that inflict death by stealing the fat from their kidneys and selling it.

What these spirits have in common is that they generally appear in times of social upheaval – for example, when building projects or industries are being developed. Changes like these are explained by a belief in harmful spirits, which exist outside a community. On a practical level, this can mean that the people who are threatened feel more in touch with each other and are therefore sometimes able to resist change.

Cargo cults

Cargo cults are religious movements that are focused on obtaining material goods through religious means. Typically, they sprang up in the islands of the south-west Pacific when colonists arrived in the 19th and 20th centuries with a dazzling array of new tools, toys, and riches. The response among the indigenous islanders was to assume that this new culture had somehow been spiritually created by deities or ancestors, and hijacked by the strangers. They felt that, in time, they too would be blessed with this wealth, and constructed ritual runways and mock airports in a ceremony to bring the goods to them. Movements like this were a response to colonialism and Christianity: by combining the fundamental beliefs of island culture with new beliefs from overseas, cargo cults enabled at least parts of ancient Pacific cultures to be preserved.

The islanders sometimes find new deities among the outsiders. On Tanna Island in Vanuatu, a group of islands in the west Pacific, a cult that worships a spirit called John Frum has existed for more than 50 years. John Frum is thought to have first appeared before tribal elders in the 1930s urging them to rebel against Christian missionaries and put their faith in the old customs. During World War II, US forces landed on the island with weapons, food, and medicine – a delivery of cargo that cult members believed was the due to the spirit of John Frum. Convinced that he was an American, islanders parade in home-made US army uniforms hoping to encourage another delivery of cargo, and build ritual runways to encourage US army planes to land with more goods.

In another part of Tanna Island there is a cluster of villages whose inhabitants worship Britain's Prince Philip, the husband of the Queen, as the divine son of a mountain spirit. This belief is thought to have emerged some time in the 1960s, when Vanuatu was an Anglo-French colony known as the New Hebrides. For centuries, the villagers had believed in an ancient story about the pale-skinned son of a mountain spirit who ventured across the seas in search of a powerful bride. This legend became associated with Prince Philip: portraits showing him with the Queen hung in colonial offices and police stations.

The acceptable face of possession

Not all spirits are worshipped. Often they are greatly feared, but even these spirits can be useful. An example, in Somalia, is the sar, a type of jinn – an anthropomorphic evil spirit described in the Qur'an – that enters and possesses women. In a male-dominated society, Somalian women are in an unstable position – as many of them openly recognize. Polygyny, where a man can have more than one wife (*see* page 94), is normal and a wife can be easily divorced. Women's activities are restricted, men are frequently away from home, and the lot of a single woman is economically difficult. Sar usually possess a married woman, often when her husband is about to take another wife, and she behaves in a way that is normally impermissible. She may demand clothes, perfume, or attention and the spirit may upbraid her husband in a way that she cannot. Both husband and wife are often convinced it is the sar rather than the woman herself who is responsible for this behaviour. In *Ecstatic Religion*, the anthropologist I. M. Lewis interprets this type of spirit possession as being a socially acceptable way for women to demand more consideration and respect.

Similarly, the Hausa of West Africa treat women who are considered to be possessed with deference because the spirit requires respect. This gives the women a temporary break from their usual lowly position. A woman who often

Vine of the soul

In the Amazon basin, entering the spirit world is facilitated by drinking a brew made from the *ayahuasca* vine. The word means "vine of the soul" in the Quechua language, and also refers to a concoction of plants that is used extensively by Amazonian shamans in order to receive visions. Many peoples in the Amazon region, such as the Achuar, believe that a vision is a type of intangible object that also has a "spirit". Experiencing one is thought to lead to a deeper understanding of the day-to-day world. Past and future generations benefit from visions of the spirit world and both the community and the individual can become wiser. A vision sometimes helps a warrior to acquire a new "soul" donated by an ancestor. When he goes into battle he wants to take with him as many souls as he can, and Achuar often seek visions before a fight. This makes a warrior stronger and reminds him that he is fighting for his people.

Understanding how to prepare the brew, using the *ayahuasca* vine and other crucial ingredients, is just the start of an apprentice shaman's journey. The training is hard. Over 100 plant species have been noted in various *ayahuasca* concoctions – each plant is thought to have its own spirit, which the shaman must learn to harness if it is to be effective in ceremonies. The vine is treated reverentially and a representative segment is often kept on a platform. Before drinking the brew, the participants in a ceremony wash to cleanse themselves spiritually. Academic studies of *ayahuasca* have found that it is largely benign – and may be useful to treat addiction, depression, and anxiety disorders.

Opposite left: This green powder is *nu-nu*, a snuff made from *mapacho*, a local tobacco. Matses Indians also use *sapo* – derived from the secretions of a tree frog – to induce hunting visions and enhance physical strength.

Opposite right: A Matses man in the Amazon region of west Brazil has *nu-nu* blown up his nose by a companion.

succumbs to possession may join a healing cult – a group of women, often led by one who is barren (or has gone through the menopause) and takes on the role of a shaman. The group has been described as a refuge for wives in constantly unhappy marriages or women who find themselves alone.

The importance of magic

In many parts of the world, magic and sorcery are thought to be the cause of events that are difficult to explain. For the Dobu islanders of Papua New Guinea, success is thought to be based on powerful magic and lack of success is therefore attributed to weak magic. According to Reo Fortune, an anthropologist working in the 1960s, the Dobu have no concept of a simple accident; instead, they believe that every death and illness is caused by witchcraft.

He described how Dobu men could chant spells that lead to death or illness. If a spirit infects someone as the result of an incantation, it can be exorcized with a counterspell. A boy learns sorcery from his father, and once he has mastered the basics he must try out a spell on someone who is not a close relative. Women are said to do their magical work in spirit form while their body sleeps, but are not regarded as blameless, as the spirit works at the bidding of the conscious self.

The evil eye

The Amhara of Ethiopia are land-owning farmers who, like many people in Eurasia and Africa, believe in the evil eye – that some people can inflict harm on others, and even destroy them, with a single glance. They live alongside the Buda, who are of a different ethnic origin. The Buda are skilled craftsmen, such as potters, blacksmiths, or weavers, and all of them are said to possess the evil eye. They are believed to be envious of the Amhara and may use their eye on them – in particular, on the most wealthy and beautiful members of the tribe. Alternatively, it is said that a Buda can shape-shift into a hyena and kill his victim by fixing his eye on him. The Buda are also said to have the magical ability to remove the victim from his grave, resealing the earth over the top so that nobody knows that the corpse is no longer there. For this reason, when an Amhara dies a member of their family watches over the grave for 40 days and 40 nights. The belief is that the body might otherwise be taken by a Buda and transported back to his house, where the dead person will be forced to work as a slave for seven years until their body finally disintegrates; if someone visits the house, the Buda is able to transform the slave into a cooking pot.

If the Amhara suspect that one of their kin is in the throes of an evil eye attack, they take them to a Christian priest or Amhara wizard. The wizard uses the blade of a hot knife to burn a specific pattern on the victim's face. As the burns heal, the pattern passes on to the face of the Buda who is responsible for the attack. If he relinquishes his victim, the family does not seek any reprisal, but if their relative dies, the Buda may be banished or killed.

Dukuns: healers and sorcerers

Java is regarded as Muslim, but the religion as practised is often a mixture of Hinduism, Islam, and the animism of traditional tribal beliefs. When someone falls ill, a number of alternative treatments are available, and they might visit a *dukun*, a healer who treats specific pains such as toothache and more general illnesses. *Dukuns* divide these general illnesses into three types. "Dirty blood" is the result eating bad food or being continually angry, jealous, or greedy. Its symptoms are a "dark mind" or general sluggishness and lethargy. Dirty blood can be followed by "lack of blood", when continuous nagging fear has depleted the patient's blood supply. Alternatively, he or she could be suffering the effects of an "empty soul" caused by a lack of spiritual discipline, such as not fasting or failing to meditate frequently. The symptoms are aimlessness and loss of strength. Occasionally, the *dukun* concludes that a sorcerer has introduced foreign objects into the patient's body. In this case their stomach would contain nails, glass, and hair, and they would show violent symptoms such as vomiting copiously and bleeding.

Dukuns are healers, but they are also thought to be sorcerers who, for payment, can inflict serious illness, or even death, on someone. The victim's only defence is to enlist the help of another *dukun*. The two sorcerers engage in a mystical struggle, during which they themselves remain unharmed, but their clients suffer or prosper according to which *dukun* is victorious. The struggle takes place within a half-circle of offerings. These are placed to appease the evil spirits and may include opium, incense, broken mirrors, hair, glass, nails, or other substances of which the spirits are particularly fond. The *dukun* who is attempting to cause harm concentrates his evil intent on the objects and, if he is successful in the battle between the two sorcerers, the spirits introduce them into the victim's stomach, causing sickness. Alternatively, they may put a piece of wire in one of the victim's limbs, causing paralysis. The firm belief in this phenomenon might explain the persistent, but unproven, stories of X-rays that show these artefacts in the stomachs of patients in Javanese hospitals.

Although *dukuns* are seen as being responsible for causing illness, they are not socially ostracized and nor are they thought of as being evil. It is also understood that a person might have what they consider to be a good reason to enlist their help; wanting to harm someone is usually the result of jealousy, betrayal, or hurt.

Above: A young Oromo nomad in East Africa wears a necklace with mirrors encased in leather to protect him from the evil eye. Protective talismans vary widely around the world. In Tibet and Turkey, people wear specific beads for protection, and in India kohl spots are drawn on the faces of beautiful children who are likely to cause jealousy.

Opposite left: Men in the Crater Mountain area of Papua New Guinea examine the intestine of a ring-tailed possum to discover the identity of a warrior's killer.

Opposite right: In Bolivia, the Aymara burn and bury offerings called *mesas* or *pagos* in order to placate the spirits that influence their lives. Aymara healers use herbal and magical remedies to cure their customers.

A Buda can shape-shift into a hyena and kill his victim by fixing his eye on him.

Accusations of sorcery are not made openly in Java, and it is thought that it is directed mainly at family members and close acquaintances. There is no such tolerance in other parts of the world.

Hunting for witches

The Ndembu of Zambia use divination to reveal the identity of sorcerers and witches, who they believe could otherwise threaten the whole group. If someone is ill, if there has been a death in their family, or if a couple is having reproductive problems that they may consult a diviner in order to identify the person who is responsible for their problems. Before witchcraft and witch-hunting were banned by the British colonial administration in Zambia, this consultation was held in public and everyone was able to attend. The diviner had to be skilled in determining the power balance between the village and family or his findings could be used to his detriment. If the person he unveiled as a sorcerer was someone who was supported by the majority of people, they could turn against him. Diviners have been killed by the angry kinsmen of an accused person. For this reason the consultation was often performed in the house of the chief, who offered the diviner his protection.

Many objects are used to determine the causes of witchcraft and the identity of witches, including figurines such as an effigy of a grieving man or a wooden snake with a human face. Before and after the divination, the diviner must avoid sex and certain foods. Accusations of witchcraft can be used to isolate or condemn people who are seen as not being socially acceptable. It can locate points of tension between people and be used to uphold majority opinions and morality. For similar reasons, journalists in the industrialized world often call a political or business scandal a witch-hunt.

Specialist healers

In Leyte in the Philippines, the Cebuano and Waray-Waray people do not consider that all sickness has its origins in sorcery. In Guinhangdan, an agricultural fishing village studied by the anthropologist Ethel Nurge in the mid-20th century, there were healers who specialized in different illnesses. Midwives dealt with birth, infants, and menstruation. They were female, and always had their own children. For sprains, dislocations, and breaks, a patient visited a masseuse or masseur, who was someone who was born feet first, possibly because the feet appearing before the head meant that the infant would grow up to be a suitable healer of limbs. Anyone who was bitten by a snake or insect, or injured by the spines of a fish, saw a *parasona*, an expert in bites, who usually came from a family that specialized in this type of healing. All these healers treated illnesses that were thought to be the result of natural events and accidents. More serious illnesses were said to be caused by spirits, witches, or sorcerers.

In this culture, sorcerers are thought to use the hair or clothes of their prospective victims to inflict death or illness on enemies or on unfaithful or reluctant lovers. Witches are said to have originally been human but to have acquired supernatural power, and they live among villagers in the shape of men or women; they can transform themselves into animals such as dogs or cats. Witches do not cause sickness, but they do prey on the weak. It is believed that they may grasp and crumple a mother's vagina, leading to her death after childbirth, or pull on the umbilical cord, causing the death of the infant.

Spirits, known as *cahaynon*, are thought to live in trees. They are invisible, but can take the form of Europeans. They normally leave humans alone and sometimes even offer their help. It is said that if someone affronts the *cahaynon*

Voodoo and black magic

Voodoo, when a sorcerer instructs evil spirits to enter a person's head, causing their death, has its origins in West Africa, from where it spread to Haiti and elsewhere in the Caribbean. In Haiti it is believed that humans are in possession of two souls. If voodoo is used, a *loa* spirit moves into the head of the person at whom it is directed, displacing one of their two souls, and the victim falls into a trembling trance. Someone who wants to protect against *loa* can do so only by making a formal proposal of marriage to another *loa* spirit, who then protects them.

A similar practice of black magic occurs in belief systems in other parts of the world, from Australia and the islands of the Pacific to South America. After a complex series of rituals to determine who is causing problems for an individual or a community, a sorcerer accuses and publicly condemns the person – making a voodoo sign towards them that shows everyone (including the victim) that their death is imminent. Cases have been reported worldwide where a previously healthy person has deteriorated rapidly and died within one or two days of being cursed. Walter B Cannon recorded a number of them in 'Voodoo Death', in 1942 (*see* page 189).

In one of the reports, a traveller to the Lower Niger in 1906 described how a man who had been given the voodoo curse "believed himself to be bewitched; no nourishment or medicines that were given to him had the slightest effect either to check the mischief or to improve his condition in any way, and nothing was able to divert him from a fate which he considered inevitable. In the same way, and under very similar conditions, I have seen Kru-men and others die in spite of every effort that was made to save them, simply because they had made up their minds, not (as we thought at the time) to die, but that being in the clutch of malignant demons they were bound to die."

In another report, from Australia, Dr Lambert from the Rockefeller Foundation recorded the experience of a Dr P S Clarke, who was working on the sugar plantations of north Queensland. "One day a Kanaka came to his hospital and told him he would die in a few days because a spell had been put upon him and nothing could be done to counteract it. The man had been known to Dr Clarke for some time. He was given a very thorough examination, including an examination of the stool and the urine. All was found normal, but as he lay in bed he gradually grew weaker. Dr Clarke called upon the foreman of the Kanakas to come to the hospital to give the man assurance, but on reaching the foot of the bed, the foreman leaned over, looked at the patient, and then turned to Dr Clarke saying, 'Yes, doctor, close up him he die' (ie, he is nearly dead). The next day, at 11 o'clock in the morning, he ceased to live. A postmortem examination showed no cause of death."

Dr Lambert also reported a case that had a happier outcome. In this example, a man called Rob was brought to a hospital in north Queensland; he was extremely weak and seriously ill, but with no obvious symptoms of pain or disease. It was discovered that he had been pointed at with a bone, indicating his immediate death. The person who had pointed it was persuaded to see Rob: "He leaned over Rob's bed and told the sick man that it was all a mistake, a mere joke – indeed, that he had not pointed a bone at him at all. The relief, Dr Lambert testifies, was almost instantaneous; that evening Rob was back at work, quite happy again, and in full possession of his physical strength."

Various theories have been put forward to explain why people die as a result of a voodoo curse or black magic. One is that the fear of being dead can itself be enough to cause death. The nervous and hormonal systems go into overdrive, leading to irregular heartbeats and the collapse of some veins; this, coupled with exhaustion, and the failure to eat or drink, results in the patient dying.

Top: A voodoo practitioner in Port-au-Prince, Haiti, places a candle on a drawing that represents the *loa* spirits. Voodoo has deep roots in Haiti – over half the population are thought to perform its rituals in some form, and often combine voodoo beliefs with those of other religions.

Left: The Dankoly Shrine in Doyissa, Benin, is dedicated solely to the cursing of enemies. The shrine is made predominantly of glass shards, oil, bones, and feathers, and voodoo devotees travel there only when in dire need of assistance.

Right: A voodoo *legba* statue in Benin protects fishermen from malevolent spirits.

in any way the spirits cause him or her to fall ill, or even die. Symptoms such as skin diseases, infections, and general aches and pains are believed to be the work of cahaynon, who are punishing their victim for an offence such as not respecting the tree in which they live. The patient must then seek one of two healers skilled in exorcizing spirits and curing supernatural diseases: the haplasan, who cures by anointing; or the taplasan, who uses medicine and incantation. If he or she is cured, this is attributed to the intervention of the supernatural world or God. If they are not cured, this is due to either a misdiagnosis or the power of the spirits.

Tribal medicines

Although illness and death are often attributed to sorcery or witchcraft, and rituals and magic are therefore part of the healing process, indigenous people around the world have also made extensive use of their environment to provide them with treatments. Many of the drugs used in the West were developed from this folk knowledge. Quinine, which is used in the treatment of malaria, was used for centuries by the Quechua-speaking peoples of the Andes who once formed the mighty Inca nation. Countries like Australia and the Philippines have passed national laws to protect local genetic resources. These laws establish that tribes and communities have some ownership over the biological resources of their region, and their knowledge about healing plants, which has sometimes been acquired over centuries. This gives them the right to share in profits made by the sale of these plants and knowledge.

> Sorcerers are thought to use the hair or clothes of their prospective victims to inflict death or illness on enemies or on unfaithful or reluctant lovers.

Medicinal plants are of great interest to the international pharmacological and cosmetics industry. First, in developed nations there is a rising incidence of allergies to chemical drugs; and second, plant-based cures have been successful. Prospecting for the plants is widespread in developing countries. This is sometimes illegal and there have been cases where they have been smuggled over borders. In particularly biodiverse regions, such as the Amazon basin, where tribal peoples know a great deal about the properties of plants, communities are at risk of losing any patent rights to this knowledge. International trade agreements define intellectual property as that which is developed by a corporation or an individual – but there is no mention of intellectual property developed by a community or tribe.

A global market

Currently a number of tribal medicinal products are entering the global market. Hoodia gordonii is a succulent plant used by the San of the Kalahari Desert as an appetite- and thirst-suppressant. It thrives in high temperatures and takes years to mature. The San take it to facilitate their method of endurance hunting, which involves running down prey over many days. Hoodia also induces a mild euphoria. It has no known side effects, and research has shown that it contains a molecule that fools a person's brain into believing they are full. Previously unknown, the molecule has been christened P 57. The licence to use it was sold to a Cambridgeshire bio-pharmaceutical company, Phytopharm, who in turn sold the development and marketing rights to the giant Pfizer Corporation. A South African lawyer, Roger Chennells, negotiated San royalties for the sale.

A rainforest tonic

The guaraná is a plant indigenous to the Amazon basin that is a popular ingredient in energy drinks and herbal weight-loss remedies, and has been used by tribal peoples in the Americas for many centuries. South American tribes (especially the Guaranis, after whom the plant was named) dry and roast its seeds and mix them with water to make a paste. This is used to prepare various foods, drinks, and medicines. Rainforest tribes take *guaraná* mainly as a stimulant and as an astringent for treating chronic diarrhoea.

European researchers began studying *guaraná* in the 1940s, and today it is taken as a health tonic by millions of Brazilians. It has also been used to reduce cellulite and as an ingredient in hair-loss products. Eighty per cent of the world's commercial production of *guaraná* paste is in the middle of the Amazon rainforest in northern Brazil; it is still made by the Guarani, who wild-harvest the seeds and process them by hand. Since 1980, FUNAI (the National Indian Foundation) has set up a number of projects to improve the local production of *guaraná*. Many cooperatives in the rainforest now support indigenous tribal economies by harvesting and producing the plant.

Nature's antibiotics

Doctors in the late 1960s were surprised when they found that members of previously uncontacted tribes in Borneo were resistant to some antibiotics. But this is not surprising. Antibiotics are simply toxins that are either disruptive or fatal to bacteria, and because they are found naturally all over the world, humans have always been able to treat bacterial infections by eating and drinking certain foods. Allicin is present in garlic and onions. Benzoic acid is found in the urogenital gland of the beaver, and erythrin is in red blood cells, and therefore in raw meat and blood, as consumed by the Masai of Kenya. Kojic acid is present in rice mould, lysozyme occurs in egg albumen, and phloetin is found in apples; even human urine has an antibacterial capacity. Nubian beer is rich in tetracycline, which is found in mould-like bacteria in the soil in which the grain grows; the brewing process increases its effectiveness.

Responding to stress

Tribal peoples, like those in the industrialized world, may be affected as much by emotional stress as they are by physical illness. Responses to this are often culturally conditioned, as in the extreme case of deaths that result from voodoo curses or black magic (*see* page 172). In Kenya, Samburu warriors respond to tension and danger by falling into a trance and shaking. This often happens during initiation rites – and has also been recorded when the men are in urban and military situations. In China, patients usually present psychological problems as physical illnesses, and Chinese medicine treats mental problems through the body; practices such as acupuncture, based on balancing the elements of the body, have been shown to reduce pain, anxiety, and stress in Western contexts. Robert Kugelmann, in an anthology of essays, *The Anthropology of Medicine*, suggested that people in the industrialized world are addicted to stress, and need it to feel busy, important, and needed. The numerous stress-management techniques introduced into businesses allow people to cope with stress rather than get rid of it, which is the aim of many traditional treatments.

Arctic hysteria

In the Arctic, there is a phenomenon called Arctic hysteria, or *pibloktoq*, which can affect just one person or become an epidemic. Sometimes it is "kayak fright", when a hunter, usually in a dangerous situation, is overwhelmed by the fear that he has been abandoned. Women who are affected run about on the ice, screaming and naked. There have been many explanations for this kind of behaviour, not

Opposite top: A *Hoodia gordonii* plant in Namibia. *Hoodia* has long been used by the San to suppress appetite on hunting trips, and may have several commercial applications.

Opposite bottom: *Guaraná*, a plant of the Amazon basin, is used medicinally by rainforest tribes who now produce *guaraná* paste to sell in the Brazilian market.

Below: *Ndokuna* is the name the Samburu of Kenya use for the fits of hysteria and violent shaking that sporadically affect their warriors. *Ndokuna* becomes more common in times of tension – in the case of this young man, in the days leading up to his circumcision. The fits last for only a few minutes, but can leave a man exhausted for hours once they have passed.

least the fact that Inuit may endure months of winter darkness on a frozen ocean, which is often silent. Also, they are not expected to repress their needs and fears, so terror can be expressed as hysterical excitement rather than depression. An Inuit shaman uses hysteria when he is possessed by another shaman with whom he is engaged in a cosmic battle. This can be contagious, and spectators often become ecstatic, much as they do in rituals such as speaking in tongues.

Divination and disease

Among the Hehe of Tanzania, traditional African psychiatrists have a pharmacological approach to mental illnesses – they treat them with medicines that have been proved to be effective. Scientific empiricism can emerge even within a supernatural belief system. Hehe psychiatrists treat only illnesses of the brain and mind, and refer anything else to another healer. They regard some diseases, like epilepsy, as being treatable with their medicines. Other problems, such as brain damage, are classified as untreatable. To diagnose an illness, the Hehe psychiatrist questions the patient extensively, then carries out a process of divination to determine whether the cause is natural or supernatural. He sometimes uses copious amounts of cannabis during the questioning, the smoke of which is inhaled by the patient, allowing him or her to relax and discuss their problems more freely. Once the diagnosis has been made, the psychiatrist might purge the patient with a strong emetic and, after they have vomited profusely, administer a pharmacological preparation. The patient is then left to sleep deeply.

In many parts of Africa, similar types of treatment have resulted in people recovering rapidly, and perhaps completely, from what seem to be intractable psychotic conditions. As with some psychiatric approaches in the industrialized West, medicinal treatments may be combined with discussions that involve members of the patient's social group or they can be treated just with medicines.

The placebo effect?

It has been suggested that it is not the medicine itself that is effective in curing a patient, but that he or she recovers simply because of the experience of being treated. This is described as the placebo effect, and is widely seen in Western medicine: for example, sugar pills are as effective in treating some mental disorders as a powerful cocktail of drugs. It has also been observed in heart surgery. In the treatment of angina, veins are re-routed to increase the flow of blood to the heart. Yet, even when the re-routing is unsuccessful, the surgery is effective: the patient reports good health and a reduction of pain. Something about the surgery works – even when it doesn't work.

Mythology, magic, and religion provide explanations for creation, change, and misfortune, a framework of ideas that enables tribespeople to understand and interpret their environment. And through communicating with the spiritual world, members of tribes across the globe have developed rituals that fulfil their needs. These can have practical effects, such as group loyalty; they mark ceremonial rites of passage, such as initiation and death; and they also provide a means of understanding and treating illness – often in a way that is both pharmaceutically and psychologically successful.

8 The Future

There are over 150 million tribal people in Africa, the Americas, Asia, Europe, and living on islands across the Pacific. Politically, we have moved beyond the terrible history of contact described in the introduction to this book, but economically the story seems shockingly similar, with tribal rights frequently ignored if money can be made. Sadly, this means that tribes are marginalized, victimized, and impoverished. Yet, there are improvements across the globe. Tribal people are becoming involved in government and even international politics. At the inconclusive Copenhagen Summit on climate change in December 2009, indigenous people showed negotiators documentaries about the immediate impacts of climate change on their homelands and way of life. There are also new initiatives to secure land rights for tribes; and the expansion of media, particularly the internet, means tribal people have more access to information, and more opportunities for self-representation.

Tribes and the modern state

In South America, in particular, tribal people are increasingly taking part in national government. In Paraguay Margarita Mbywangi, a female chief from the Ache tribe, was made a government minister in 2008, the first indigenous person in the country to hold such a position. Other tribes in the region were worried that she would favour the Ache in her policy decisions, giving them preferential treatment, and in answer to their concerns she pledged to uphold all people's rights. Elsewhere in South America, Evo Morales, a member of the Aymara tribe and president of Bolivia since 2006, controversially claims to be the country's first indigenous leader, though other presidents have traced a tribal heritage.

Who are the land-owners?

The conflict between tribes and governments often comes down to one question: Who owns the land? Although the Mapuche in southern Chile filed lawsuits in attempt to prevent the construction of a hydroelectric dam on the Bío Bío River, these were ultimately futile. Five hundred people

Previous page:
A Masai woman in Magadi, Kenya, casts her vote in the nation's closest-ever presidential race, in December 2007.

Opposite: Chairman Marcus Levings of North Dakota puts a question to President Obama during an interactive discussion that the President held with tribal leaders in 2009.

Right: An aboriginal man in Arhnem Land, Australia, calls his clan to a *corroboree* at Korlobidahdah. Newly installed telephones have vastly improved communications across the outback. Previously, aboriginal communities used wind-up radio phones that necessitated callers talking loudly to make themselves heard over others.

from the Mapuche-Pehuenche communities were forcibly relocated and for them the new millennium began with the flooding of their ancestral lands. Sadly, this is a story that is repeated the world over. Despite the UN Declaration of Human Rights in 1948, the right of indigenous people to remain on their land is often overlooked in favour of "national interests".

Oil disputes: a new solution?

In Ecuador a solution has been proposed that would allow tribal peoples to stay on the land where they have lived for millennia. The Yasuni area of the Amazon basin, a region that is thought to have the highest biodiversity in the world, is under threat from oil prospectors. Although Yasuni has been a national park since 1979, and has even been declared a world biosphere reserve by UNESCO, oil companies have drilled in the area for the past 30 years and now want to extract the oil reserves under the Yasuni rainforest. Rafael Correa, Ecuador's president, has stated that his government would like to leave the crude oil in the ground for ever so that the Yasuni's valuable resources remain free from contamination. He has asked for wealthy nations to compensate Ecuador for half the income the country would have received from the oil – money that would be

used to protect the Yasuni area as a vital resource in the battle against climate change and habitat destruction. Protecting the forest will also protect its indigenous inhabitants, who include the Tagaeri and Taromenane – tribes who live in voluntary isolation, and could be eradicated by diseases if outsiders encroach on the forest.

In Peru, the Achuar tribe has struggled for decades with unwanted oil wells in its part of the rainforest, and has presented compelling evidence that its people have suffered terribly from their effects. FECONACO (The Federation of Native Communities of the Corrientes River) claims that for every barrel of oil produced, nine barrels of contaminated water are discharged as a by-product: more than a million barrels a day. As well as destroying the ecosystem of the forest in which the Achuar live, the oil is compromising the health of the people. The water contains high concentrations of hydrocarbons as well as heavy metals like lead, cadmium, mercury, and arsenic. These are absorbed by the fish the Achuar rely on for food. High levels of these substances are known to cause serious physical and mental illnesses, including cancer and genetic deformities. A survey carried out by Peru's Ministry of Health in 2006 found that cadmium levels in the blood of more than 98 per cent of tribespeople exceeded safe levels, and more than 66 per cent of children had worrying levels of lead in their blood.

Logging and prospecting

Despite declaring the southern area of Yasuni a no-go area, the Ecuadorian authorities have not stopped the incursions of loggers and prospectors into the region, and the Tagaeri and Taromenane have suffered from massacres in the recent past. In 2003, 14 Tagaeri were killed by loggers; and in 2006, 30 Taromenane were killed in rivalries over resources with the Hoarani, a neighbouring tribe whose members often act as guides for loggers. Ecuador now has the unenviable reputation of being a dangerous place for uncontacted tribes. Correa's possible solution offers a glimmer of hope to its indigenous peoples.

Laws and land

Indigenous leaders in North America, New Zealand, and Australia have led a movement to secure title to lands and waters through the courts. They have a strong argument, as the land was not taken from them legally in the first place. The process is not easy and can sometimes pit indigenous peoples against each other. Also, after the catastrophic disruption of European contact it can be difficult for groups who have been forced to splinter, move, and adapt to prove a continuous cultural connection to their land.

In Australia, the first landmark case was in 1971. The Yolngu of Arnhem Land sent a petition on bark to the House

The people of the whale

A battle can sometimes be for resources rather than land, and there are occasions when this results in an ethical dilemma. The Inupiat of northern Alaska, a group of the Inuit tribe, call themselves the "People of the Whale" as they have hunted the Arctic bowhead for at least 2500 years, and it is a vital part of their culture: in mythology the goddess of the whale – Sedna – is the most revered of all deities. They use every part of the animal: whale bones to build homes and sleds, entrails for packing material, oil for light and heat – and blubber is an essential food. Historically, they harvested about 60 bowheads a year from the Bering Sea. Today, stone-tipped harpoons have been replaced by guns and explosives, but the Inupiat still use seal-skin boats, known as *umiaks*, to hunt the whales.

Such hunting posed no danger to the bowhead when its population was at a naturally high level. But the balance was upset when American sailors discovered rich stocks of the whale in 1848. Commercial whaling in the Bering Sea prospered until about 1910 and drastically reduced the bowhead population, which has failed to recover despite being protected by international treaties. With low population levels, the species is vulnerable to extinction by overhunting or oil pollution – or as a result of poorly

understood spontaneous population "crashes". Currently, the Inupiat are legally permitted to hunt and kill a small number of bowhead each year. Should they be allowed to hunt them, when other peoples are not? They think so, as the practice is essential to their way of life. But many marine conservationists disagree.

Opposite: Oil pipelines run directly past an indigenous house in the Ecuadorian Amazon basin. Environmental activists across the world oppose drilling for oil in the region because of its phenomenal biodiversity. Exploitation by oil companies has had disastrous consequences for the tribal peoples of the Amazon, who are protesting against an industry that pollutes their home and leaves dangerous levels of heavy metals in the blood of many tribespeople – known to lead to cancers and genetic deformities.

of Representatives protesting against a plan to exile them from their land to make way for a bauxite mine. It resulted in a parliamentary inquiry that recommended the Yolngu be compensated – the first-ever recognition that indigenous Australians had legal rights to where they lived. However, there was no decision to return the land, so the Yolngu took the case up to the Supreme Court of the Northern Territory. Sadly, they were unsuccessful in preventing mining on their land. The presiding judge ruled that native title was not part of the law of Australia and any native title rights were therefore not recognizable. Although the Yolngu lost the case, it motivated a campaign that native title should be recognized, and after two long decades this was finally successful. Also, the judge had recognized the validity of oral evidence to establish property rights, normally inadmissible because written evidence is required, but a vital precondition for a successful land rights case for tribal people without a written history.

Messages and the media

Portraying tribal people in the national and international media is fraught with difficulty, and is open to charges of misrepresentation. This is usually because the cameraman, journalist, or photographer is an outsider and often conveys, explicitly or implicitly, his or her own views about a tribe's culture.

Nanook of the North, a silent film made in the 1920s, and the first feature-length documentary, showed the life of an Inuit, Nanook, and his family in the Canadian Arctic as they hunted, fished, and built igloos. It brought the customs of the Inuit, and the way they lived, to the attention of a wider world and met with great success in North America and abroad. However, after this initially positive reaction its director, Robert Flaherty, faced criticism for staging some of the sequences. Although "Nanook" (it later transpired that this was not his real name) usually hunted with a gun, Flaherty encouraged him to use traditional Inuit weapons in order to give the audience what he assumed they wanted to see. (In fact, in the film Nanook hunted successfully with a spear, suggesting that he had used one before.) Flaherty was also condemned for ending the documentary with the suggestion that the family were at risk of dying if they did not soon find a shelter. In reality, there were French-Canadian and Inuit settlements near to where *Nanook of the North* was being shot. Some of the acted elements in the film were perhaps understandable, given that the combination of Flaherty's cumbersome equipment and the extreme weather conditions made it necessary to shoot scenes as quickly as possible.

Above: A still from Robert Flaherty's *Nanook of the North* shows "Nanook" hunting with a traditional spear, rather than his usual gun.

Similar controversies often follow other films about tribes. *The Disappearing World* series, produced in the United Kingdom by Granada Television, and screened from 1970 to 1977, was criticized by some anthropologists who described it as reductionist and inadequate. They argued that in each episode there was never enough time to understand and explain unfamiliar customs and behaviours, and that as a result the audience was presented with a romanticized version of the "noble savage" – the idea, inherent in the Romantic philosophy of the 18th and 19th centuries, that the "natural man" encountered by Europeans in the Americas was an innocent example of humanity in its pure state, untouched by the corrupting influence of civilization. This idea was revolutionary at a time when many people in Europe considered uncivilized "savages" to be inferior to themselves, but has been hugely criticized in the 20th century as being condescending, racist, and incorrect as it denies tribal people their own culture, and suggests they are akin to animals living in a "natural" state.

The audience was presented with a romanticized version of the "noble savage".

Tribe, a popular BBC2 series screened worldwide from 2005 to 2007, and, like the *Disappearing World* series, also produced in the United Kingdom, faced similar criticism. The presenter, Bruce Parry, lived with indigenous people, participating in their rituals, sharing their food, and sleeping in their huts; a small crew filmed the results. Some dismissed the series – a reviewer in *The Times* said it was "obscene post-colonial pygmy tourism masquerading as eco-entertainment" – but in a statement to *New Scientist* magazine, Survival International, the biggest charity campaigning for tribal peoples, asserted that, "the Tribe programmes bring tribal peoples vividly to life" and, furthermore, that "public awareness and the force of public opinion are absolutely crucial

Opposite: Aboriginal cultures and languages are given a media platform in Australia, where the aboriginal radio network covers one-fifth of the country. This is the crew of Australia's first aboriginal station, outside their studio in Alice Springs.

in ensuring that tribal peoples' rights are respected". An interesting avenue for subsequent research could be to investigate what the tribespeople themselves got out of the media experience, and how – if at all – the programmes have changed their lives.

New opportunities

Some tribal communities have been given the opportunity to broadcast programmes that follow their own agenda. APTN (a Canadian television station created in 1999) is dedicated to content from indigenous peoples; most of this comes from Canada, with 30 per cent supplied by tribes in other countries. As most of these communities have little representation in, or access to, programming, this is a great example of how mass media can empower minority groups. In Australia, a network of over 125 licensed indigenous radio stations spans the country. There are stations in remote desert areas and also in major cities such as Melbourne, where one started broadcasting in 2003. Radio stations allow tribal cultures and languages to maintain their identities: 5NPY represents the tribal peoples of the Anangu Pitjantjatjara lands and broadcasts from 11 aboriginal communities in south Australia. This allows their cultures to flourish independently, but also to be part of a radio network that covers more than one-fifth of Australia's landmass.

> In Australia, a network of over 125 licensed indigenous radio stations spans the country.

The internet enables tribal peoples to communicate their identity and campaigns globally. Because its control is mainly in the hands of the digitized English-speaking West, there is a worry that it could be a tool for further rapid colonization and acculturation. However, when local champions of the internet adapt the technology for tribal peoples, it offers some great opportunities for them. The Achuar of Peru maintain a website that shows their material culture in a way that is more accessible than illustrations in an anthropological book or exhibits in a museum gallery, and also gives details about the Achuars' protest

against oil companies. The website of the Centre for World Indigenous Studies has over 30,000 documents in an online library that is a leading source of information on contemporary indigenous issues; and www.peoplink.org works through non-profit organizations to provide internet training and websites for more than 100,000 indigenous artists and manufacturers in 20 countries. This enables a potter in Bangladesh to sell ceramics to a businessman in Tokyo, and allows a couple in Berlin to search for a village-run rainforest tour (*see also* Resources, page 188). In the Canadian Arctic, the province of Nunavut has even been developing a computer code to enable its geographically far-flung government offices to communicate with each other using a common Inuktitut language.

Tourism: a delicate balancing act

Tourism can have both positive and negative effects on tribes. It can provide an income, and allow indigenous people to showcase their culture and teach others about how they live. Conversely, it can result in exploitation, particularly when a tribal way of life is presented as a sensational spectacle and there is little opportunity for tribespeople to interact with others on their own terms.

In Tanzania, cultural tourism is an increasing draw in a country that already boasts the Serengeti National Park, Kilimanjaro, and the nearby island of Zanzibar as natural attractions. It generates over $700 million per year and the main attraction is the colourfully adorned, proud, and beautiful Masai. Until 50 years ago, this nomadic tribe roamed the Ngorongoro crater and the Serengeti plains. Their cattle grazed alongside giraffe, zebra, and impala. In 1959, the Masai were

Opposite: A young tourist meets a Masai man. The tribal cultures of Kenya and Tanzania have become significant draws for tourists. Encounters between tribespeople and visitors are often managed by hotels, restaurants, or safari lodges, where warriors perform dances. In recent years, the Masai have shown a desire to develop their own tourism, which would enable them to meet visitors on their own terms and receive more of the profits.

Above left: A Masai man in Tanzania stands next to a dead cow, one of 3000–4000 cattle that died in the last months of 2009. Many Masai have been unable to remain on their lands and have travelled to cities like Arusha in a desperate search for work and food. Indigenous people are often on the front line of climate change and can drastically suffer its effects.

Above right: A child of the remote Turkana tribe in northern Kenya digs a hole in a river bed to find water. Diminishing water levels mean that children have to dig deeper and deeper, and many have been killed when the walls of the holes collapse on them. Over 23 million people in East Africa face a critical shortage of food and water, and recent repeated droughts are worsening the situation.

evicted from their best pastures on the Serengeti, and, 16 years later, from the Ngorongoro crater. Although they had been successful custodians of the wildlife on their lands, these evictions were said to be for the purposes of conservation. As a result, the Masai had to graze more cattle on other parts of Masailand, which has degraded the pasture and subsequently reduced the wildlife levels in these areas. The land they once roamed is used by tourists to view animals, and the Masai, who often don't stay in school for long because educational opportunities are limited, are usually employed as security guards or porters.

The best way for them to make money has been to open their villages to tourists, and some Masai have created homesteads so that visitors can stay overnight and experience their culture at first-hand. Backpackers, volunteers, and regular holiday-makers have visited these villages and, in doing so, contributed directly to the community's pockets. But the Masai face government opposition to their entrepreneurism, and have battled against plans to impose a punitive tax on their income from this scheme. They argue that it is as if the government does not want them to meet visitors directly.

Climate change

Tribes are on the front line of the battle to adapt to climate change. Indigenous people contribute very little to greenhouse gases, but changing temperatures and weather patterns, at least some of which are likely to be the result of emissions from the industrial world, are posing a threat to the survival of tribal communities worldwide.

In Kenya, severe droughts in the first decade of the new millennium endangered the lives of many Kenyans, including the Masai. During these, the Masai have reported huge population crashes in animal species, including zebras and monkeys, and pastoralists have rapidly lost cattle, their main and often their only livelihood. These are not only a source of nutrition and income; they are also essential to Masai culture, and without them it is impossible to make dowry payments and establish kin relationships in the traditional way. Masai elders have reported that the drought that began in 2006 was beyond the understanding and experience of their people, and has resulted in a difficult struggle to stay alive.

Further north, Inuit communities are being displaced as hunting territories dwindle or disappear because of the melting of the polar ice. In Nordic countries, the Sami are experiencing a northward-moving tree line and changing animal migration patterns. Sami University College is carrying out research into how to use native ecological knowledge in order to adapt to change, recognizing that indigenous peoples have previous experience of shifts in environmental patterns that are of benefit to them, and possibly also to other groups. Throughout India, Adivasi (Indian indigenous tribespeople) communities are using their traditional knowledge to develop drought-resistant varieties of crops and protection against floods.

Taking action

In today's world, it is necessary to worry about what the future holds for tribal peoples. In 2007, the United Nations General Assembly adopted the United Nations Declaration on the Rights of Indigenous Peoples. It was a positive step that acknowledged the needs of tribes, but it was not legally binding for member states, and tribal rights are being breached by individuals, corporations, and governments. However, despite this, and in spite of the threats posed by climate change, there is always hope. If indigenous peoples were not adaptable and innovative, there would be far fewer surviving tribes.

There is also help from the industrialized world (*see* Resources, page 188), in the form of non-governmental organizations, and charities such as the commendable Survival International who work on behalf of tribal people across the globe. Other worldwide campaigns, such as those run by the World Wildlife Fund and Greenpeace, aim to preserve the wilderness areas in which tribes live. The support for these campaigns to ensure the future of tribes is increasing as the number of people who believe that tribal societies are worth preserving grows. Uncontacted tribes need help to keep others off their land if they are to remain isolated, or must be enabled to interact with outsiders on their own terms. Indigenous peoples who are already in contact with the industrialized world require strong advocacy in courts and governments; and it is essential that money donated by the West goes directly into the pockets of tribal communities.

People who care about the survival of tribes can, through politics, media, or ethical consumption, show solidarity with indigenous peoples, add momentum to their struggle for rights, and, in extreme cases, join them in their fight for survival. If we care enough about tribal peoples to write or read books about them, we surely want to be part of a world where they can exist. In our own way, all of us can try to make this happen.

If indigenous peoples weren't adaptable and innovative there would be far fewer surviving tribes.

Opposite: Tribal groups in Brazil often take to the streets in protest. Here they are campaigning on a range of issues, including the lack of accessible health care for remote tribes that suffer hugely from malaria and epidemics of introduced diseases.

Resources and Further Reading

If you want to research the lives of tribal peoples further, the following resources are a good starting point.

www.piersgibbon.com/tribes has links where you can find out more about campaigns to help tribal people, as well as videos and radio interviews that relate to the topics covered in the book.

CULTURES AND COMMUNICATION

The internet is a valuable tool for providing information about indigenous cultures, and enabling them to communicate with the industrialized world.

www.achuarperu.org/en/index.htm showcases the art, language, and dress of the Achuar of Peru, and details the tribe's protest against oil companies.

www.cwis.org the website of the Centre for World Indigenous Studies is devoted to indigenous cultures, and has over 30,000 documents in an online library.

www.peoplink.org works through non-profit organizations to provide internet training and their own websites for more than 100,000 indigenous artists and manufacturers in 20 countries.

ECOLOGICAL TRAVEL

The following websites are useful for anyone who is travelling abroad and wants to act responsibly towards indigenous peoples:

Tourism Concern (www.tourismconcern.org.uk) has organized human rights campaigns, and campaigns against abuse in the name of tourism.

www.planeta.com is the world's largest ecotourism website with accurate, insightful information about tourism in Latin America.

Fair Trade Tourism is an exciting concept for concerned travellers, and South Africa Fair Trade Tourism (www.fairtourismsa.org.za) is currently one of the leaders in this field. Instead of focusing solely on economic development, fair trade provides a framework for fair economics and human rights.

Global Exchange (www.globalexchange.org) is an international organization that offers insightful tours.

Exodus (www.exodus.co.uk) and Himalayan High Treks (www.himalayanhightreks.com) are smaller adventure companies that support community education and social projects in the areas they visit.

The Third World Network (www.twnside.org.sg/tour.htm) and the International Center for Responsible Tourism (www.icrtourism.org) offer more valuable information.

MUSEUMS

Ethnographic museums worldwide have a vast collection of tribal culture material, and many museums run programmes that collaborate with tribal peoples. Two examples of larger museums are the Peabody Museum of Yale, Connecticut, www.peabody.yale.edu, which runs events for a number of Native American communities, and the Museum of Aboriginal Culture in Cuenca, Ecuador, which represents 11 different indigenous cultures of Ecuador. There are also many small community-led museums around the world, such as the Suquamish Museum and Cultural Centre in Port Madison Indian Reservation.

CHARITIES

The following charities campaign on behalf of indigenous peoples:

Survival International (www.survivalinternational.org) run a letter-writing campaign that really brings results. People from all over the world contact governments on behalf of under-represented tribal peoples. Survival also run a series of focused lobbying and fundraising campaigns on behalf of tribal peoples.

Forest Peoples (www.forestpeoples.org) is dedicated to championing the rights of tribes living in rainforests, including uncontacted groups in the Amazon region and West Papua.

The Tribes Foundation (www.the-tribes-foundation.org) in the United Kingdom acts to relieve the poverty faced by indigenous peoples.

MAGAZINES AND JOURNALS

The Good Alternative Travel Guide and *Community Based Tourism Handbook*, both published by Tourism Concern, provide information on choosing a travel destination.

New Internationalist (www.newint.org) often publishes articles and books about issues faced by indigenous people.

National Geographic (www.national-geographic-magazine.co.uk) frequently includes articles about tribal peoples.

Academic journals of anthropological study include the quarterly publication *American Anthropologist* (www.aaanet.org/publications/ameranthro.cfm), *Current Anthropology* (http://www.journals.uchicago.edu/toc/ca/current), and the *Journal of the Royal Anthropological Institute* (www.wiley.com/bw/journal.asp?ref=1359-0987).

BOOKS

Below is a list of books that gives some suggestions for further reading in the field of anthropology. It is not a comprehensive bibliography, as information for this book was also obtained from other publications including websites and newspapers, and reflects personal knowledge and communications.

General

Beatties, J H M, *Nyoro Marriage and Affinity*, 1958
Descola, Philippe, *Spears of Twilight*, 1996
Digard, Jean Pierre, 'The Bakhtiari', in Richard Tapper and Jon Thompson (eds), *The Nomadic Peoples of Iran*, 2002
Evans-Pritchard, E E, *The Nuer*, 1940

Haley, Alex, *Roots*, 1976

Hallgren, Claes, *Two Travellers – Two Pictures of Australia*, 2003

Hoffman, Katherine, *We Share Walls*, 2007

Liedloff, Jean, *The Continuum Concept*, 1975

Malinowski, Bronislaw, *Argonauts of the Western Pacific*, 1940

Viollet-le-Duc, Eugène-Emmanuel, *The Habitations of Man in All Ages*, 1876

Westermarck, Edward, *The History of Human Marriage*, 1891

1 Food and Drink

Arens, William, *The Man-Eating Myth*, 1979

Arnott, Margaret L (ed), *Gastronomy: the Anthropology of Food and Food Habits*, 1975

Bodenheimer, F S, *Insects as Human Food*, 1951

Counihan, Carole M, *The Anthropology of Food and Body: Gender, Meaning, and Power*, 1999

Douglas, Mary (ed), *Constructive Drinking: Perspectives on Drink from Anthropology*, 1987

Kuper, Jessica (ed), *The Anthropologist's Cookbook*, 1977

2 Dress and Adornment

Brain, Robert, *The Decorated Body*, 1979

Craik, J, *The Face of Fashion*, 1994

Eicher, Joanne B (ed), *Dress and Ethnicity*, 1995

El Guindi, Fadwa, *Veil: Modesty, Privacy, and Resistance*, 1999

Heiser, Charles B, *The Gourd Book*, 1979

Rieff Anawalt, Patricia, *The Worldwide History of Dress*, 2007

3 House, Shelter, Home

Carsten, J and Hugh-Jones, S, *About the House: Levi-Strauss and Beyond*, 1995

Dethier, Jean, *Down to Earth: Mud Architecture; An Old Idea, a New Future*, 1982

Duly, Colin, *The Houses of Mankind*, 1979

Fox, James J, *Inside Austronesian Houses: Perspectives on Domestic Designs for Living*, 1993

Hirschman, Stephanie (series ed), *Tents: Shelters, Homes, and Ways of Life*, 1988

Oliver, Paul, *Dwellings*, 2003

Oliver, Paul (ed), *Shelter, Sign, and Symbol*, 1975

Oliver, Paul (ed), *Shelter and Society*, 1976

Pile, John F, *A History of Interior Design*, 2005

Waterson, R, *The Living House: An Anthropology of Architecture in Southeast Asia*, 1990

4 Courtship and Marriage

Berreman, Gerald D, 'Pahari Polyandry', *American Anthropologist*, Vol 64(1): pages 60–74, 1962

Bohannan, Laura, 'Dahomean Marriage: A Revaluation', *Africa*, Vol 19: pages 273–87, 1949

Bohannen, Paul and Middleton, John (eds), *Marriage, Family, and Residence*, 1968

Evans-Pritchard, E E, *Kinship and Marriage Among the Nuer*, 1951

Gongh, Kathleen E, 'The Nayars and the Definition of Marriage', *The Journal of the Royal Anthropological Institute*, Vol 89(1): pages 23–34, 1959

Goody, Jack, 'A Comparative Approach to Incest and Adultery', *British Journal of Sociology*, Vol 7 No. 4: pages 286–305, 1956

Mair, Lucy, *Marriage*, 1971

Malinowski, Bronislaw, *Sex, Culture, and Myth*, 1962

Smith, M G 'Secondary Marriage in Northern Nigeria', *Africa*, Vol 23 No. 4: pages 298–323, 1953

5 Music, Dance, Leisure

Bauman, Richard (ed), *Folklore, Cultural Performances, and Popular Entertainments*, 1992

Brenneis, Donald, 'Grog and Gossip in Bhatgaon', *American Ethnologist*, Vol 11(3): pages 487–506, 1984

Falkener, Edward, *Games Ancient and Oriental and How to Play Them*, 1892

Finnegan, Ruth, *Oral Poetry*, 1977

Hart, M, *Drumming at the Edge of Magic*, 1992

Hartland, Edwin Sidney, *The Science of Fairytales*, 1891

Wells, Robin E, *An Introduction to the Music of the Basotho*, 1994

Welsford, Enid, *The Fool*, 1935

6 Social Structures, War, Peace

Bohannan, Paul (ed), *Law and Warfare*, 1967

Cohen, Ronald and Middleton, John (eds), *Comparative Political Systems*, 1967

Feest, Christian, *The Art of War*, 1980

Hamnet, Ian, *Social Anthropology and Law*, 1977

Malinowski, Bronislaw, *Crime and Custom in Savage Society*, 1926

7 Belief, Ritual, Healthcare

Cannon, Walter B, 'Voodoo Death', *American Anthropologist*, 44: pages 169–81, 1942

Davies, Jon (ed), *Ritual and Remembrance*, 1994

Hartland, Edwin Sidney, *Ritual and Belief: Studies in the History of Religion*, 1914

Huntingdon, R and Metcalf, P, *Celebrations of Death*, 1991

Landy, David (ed), *Culture, Disease, and Healing*, 1977

Lewis, I M, *Ecstatic Religion*, 1971

Middleton, John (ed), *Myth and Cosmos*, 1967

Romanucci-Ross, Lola, Moermann, Daniel E, and Tancredi, Laurence R (eds), *The Anthropology of Medicine From Culture to Method*, 1991

Voogelbreinder, Snu, *Garden of Eden*, 2009

This page: Himba women and a child walk across an exposed desert plain in the Kunene region of Namibia.

Index

Page numbers in *italic* refer to illustrations

Picture Credits and Acknowledgements

Africa Image Library/Ariadne Van Zandbergen 116 left, 116 bottom right. **Alamy**/AfriPics.com 54; /Bryan and Cherry Alexander/Arcticphoto 57 bottom left, 70, 152; /Amanda Ahn/dbimages 90–1; /Archives du 7eme Art/Photos 12 182; /Asia Images Group Pte Ltd 75; /Bill Bachman 21 bottom left; /Louise Batalla Duran 172 bottom right; /Carol Beckwith and Angela Fisher/Robert Estall Photo Agency 163 top centre; /Susanna Bennett 21 top left; /Suzy Bennett 21 top right; /blickwinkel/Dolder 9 top centre right; /blickwinkel/Igelmund 102; /blickwinkel/Katz 80 top left; /blickwinkel/McPHOTO/ZAD 20, 188–9; /blickwinkel/Rocker 150–1; /Nancy Carter/North Wind Picture Archives 115; /Christine Osborne Pictures 154 left; /Dennis Cox 142; /Sue Cunningham Photographic 39 bottom; /Sue Cunningham/Worldwide Picture Library 39 top; /dbimages 40 right; /Marc Dozier/Hemis 110; /Duffour/Andia 63 top; /Bark Fahnestock 93; /Pavel Filatov 112 left; /Angela Fisher/Robert Estall Photo Agency 161 bottom, 170; /Gilad Flesch/PhotoStock–Israel 28 top left, 28 bottom left, 28 right; /Gable/Sylvia Cordaiy Photo Library Ltd 104 right; /David Gillison/Peter Arnold, Inc 171 left; /Greenshoots Communications 132; /Darren Greenwood/Design Pics Inc 6; /Darrell Gulin/Danita Delimont 116 top right; /Robin Hanbury-Tenison/Robert Harding Picture Library Ltd 103; /Cindy Miller Hopkins/DanitaDelimont.com 71; /Peter Horree 139 left, 139 right; /Roger Hutchings 53 top; /INTERFOTO 145 bottom right; /F Jack Jackson 42 bottom right; /Jack Jackson/Robert Harding Picture Library Ltd 63 bottom left; /Gavriel Jecan/Danita Delimont 53 centre; /JKimages 53 bottom; /David Keith Jones/Images of Africa Photobank 161 top, 163 bottom; /Wolfgang Kaehler 144–5; /Alan Keohane/Imagestate Media Partners Limited – Impact Photos 99 left; /Nikolay Kuznetsov/imagebroker 63 bottom right; /Robin Laurance/Imagestate Media Partners Limited – Impact Photos 123; /Tina Manley/Africa 77 right; /J Marshall – Tribaleye Images 171 right; /mediacolor's 41 left, 42 left, 42 top right; /Bruno Morandi/Robert Harding Picture Library Ltd 67 top left; /Brian Moser/Hutchison Archive/Eye Ubiquitous 38; /Pete Oxford/Danita Delimont 8 top right; /Colin Roy Owen 174 top; /Edward Parker 79; /Nigel Pavitt/John Warburton-Lee Photography 101 left, 160 bottom right, 161 centre; /Lincoln Potter/Danita Delimont 57 top left; /Louis-Marie Preau/Hemis 27 right; /Robert Harding Picture Library Ltd 50 centre; /Robert J Ross/Peter Arnold, Inc 104 centre; /Boaz Rottem 163 top left, 166 top left; /Anders Ryman 48 top left; /Howard Sayer 121; /Philip Scalia 169; /Ivan Strasburg/Hutchison Archive/Eye Ubiquitous 124–5; /Jane Sweeney/Robert Harding Picture Library 77 left; /Robin Smith/Art Directors and TRIP 75 bottom left; /Ariadne Van Zandbergen 160 left, 160 top right. **ArcticPhoto**/Bryan and Cherry Alexander 67 bottom right. **Corbis**/Peter Adams 9 top right; /Piyal Adhikary/epa 98; /Yann Arthus-Bertrand 78; /Atlantide Phototravel 48 bottom left, 172 bottom left; /Anthony Bannister/Gallo Images 22 centre right, 23; /Annie Belt 135; /Remi Benali 32, 166 top right; /Bettmann 10 bottom left, 145 top; /Christophe Boisvieux 30–1; /Richard Chung/Reuters 49; /Dean Conger 57 bottom right; /William Coupon 9 top centre left, 9 bottom left; /Margaret Courtney-Clarke 27 left; /DLILLC 34–5; /Marc Dozier/Hemis 24; /Macduff Everton 9 bottom centre right, 64, 65, 92 left; /Eyes on Asia 8 bottom right; /Owen Franken 37; /Free Agents Limited 147; /Qin Gang/XinHua/Xinhua Press 89 right; /Gianni Giansanti 26, 68; /Jacques Haillot/Sygma 8 bottom centre right; /Robin Hanbury-Tenison/Robert Harding World Imagery 40 left; /Roger De La Harpe/Gallo Images 84, 127; /Martin Harvey 104 left; /Lindsay Hebberd 9 bottom centre left, 89 centre, 101 right, 158 left; /Chris Hellier 75 top left 86; /Ollart Herve/Sygma 174 bottom; /HO/Reuters 140 bottom; /Angelo Hornak 81 top centre; /Jeremy Horner 52; /Dave G Houser 143; /Rob Howard 25; /Jon Hrusa/epa 95 top right, 95 bottom right; /Dave Hunt/epa 146 right; /Image Source 80 right; /Gavriel Jecan 8 bottom left, 8 top centre right, 166 bottom; /Peter Johnson 19, 31 right; /Manca Juvan 100 top; /Wolfgang Kaehler 8 top left; /Farahanaz Karimy/epa 92 right; /Steven Kazlowski/Science Faction 181; /Earl and Nazima Kowall 81 bottom left, 96, 112 right, 122; /Ludo Kuipers 21 bottom right; /Daniel Lainé 136 left, 136 right, 162 left, 162 right; /Otto Lang 118; /Frans Lanting 22 bottom right; /Danny Lehman 9 top left; /Charles and Josette Lenars 48 top centre, 48 top right, 48 centre left, 114, 163 top right; /Kim Ludbrook/epa 95 bottom left; /Gerd Ludwig 81 top right; /Gideon Mendel 58–9; /Kazuyoshi Nomachi 47 top left; /Richard T Nowitz 184; /Altaf Qadri/epa 14–15 bottom; /Jean-Baptiste Rabouan/Hemis 4–5, 9 bottom right; /Radius Images 81 top left; /Reuters 55 right, 89 left, 155; /Lucille Reyboz/Sygma 80 bottom left, 159 left; /Jeffrey L Rotman 168 left, 168 right; /Anders Ryman 33, 87, 128 bottom left, 128 bottom right, 133; /Ron Sachs/Pool/CNP 178; /Hamid Sardar 101 centre; /Albrecht G Schaefer 76; /Hugh Sitton 2–3, 50 right; /Frédéric Soltan 8 bottom centre left, 31 centre, 99 right, 119; /Paul A Souders 149; /George Steinmetz 81 bottom centre, 159 right; /Les Stone/Sygma 153; /STR/epa 22 top right; /Keren Su 18, 36; /Ognen Teofilovski/Reuters 100 bottom; /Alanah M Torralba/epa 156; /Penny Tweedie 117, 130–1, 154 right, 179, 183; /Vanni Archive 67 top right; /Ivan Vdovin/JAI 14–15 top; /Steven Vidler/Eurasia Press 8 top centre left; /Brian A Vikander 107 top left; /Kamran Wazir/Reuters 140 top; /Reza/Webistan 146 left; /Nathalie Weemaels/epa 180; /Michele Westmorland 108–9; /Alison Wright 41 right; /Valdrin Xhemaj/epa 85; /Michael S Yamashita 47 top right, 137, 158 right. **Getty Images**/Eitan Abramovich 172 top; /Peter Adams 126; /Apic 128 top; /Torsten Blackwood/AFP 107 top right, 107 bottom; /EVARISTO SA/AFP 187; /Christopher Furlong 185 right; /Gavin Hellier 56; /Carl Iwasaki/Time and Life Pictures 73 top, 73 bottom left, 73 bottom right; /Indranil Mukherjee/AFP 16–17; /Per-Anders Pettersson 185 left; /Herman du Plessis 45; /Mark Ralston/AFP 44; /Roberto Schmidt/AFP 176–7; /STRDEL/AFP 82–3. **Lonely Planet Images**/Eric Wheater 50 left. **National Geographic Stock**/Alaska Stock Images 129; /Gilbert M Grosvenor 22 left; /Frank and Helen Schreider 67 centre; /James L Stanfield 47 bottom left. **Newspix**/News Ltd/3rd Party Managed Reproduction and Supply Rights 10 top right. **Panos**/Caroline Penn 29. **Photolibrary Group**/Per-Andre Hoffmann 157; /Jack Jackson 47 bottom centre; /Morales Morales 164; /Nigel Pavitt 61, 165, 175; /Nigel Pavitt/John Warburton-Lee Photography 111; /Ivan Vdovin 67 bottom left; /Ariadne Van Zandbergen 60, 120. **Press Association Images**/AP 94; /Gleison Miranda, FUNAI/AP 12. **Robert Estall Photo Agency**/Angela Fisher-Carol Beckwith 55 left. **Still Pictures**/Jacques Jangoux/Peter Arnold 113 left; /Patricia Jordan/Peter Arnold 113 right; /McPHOTO/Blickwinkel 47 bottom right.

Many thanks to Jane Houston, Renée Godfrey, Leanne Bryan, Laura Price Jenny Doubt, Tessa Clark and Jo Richardson.

Thanks also to Hannah McBain, Anja Fabricius, Joanna Dodd, Philip Dodd, Mark Gibbon, Carla Octigan, my long-suffering tutors at Oxford University and to all the people who have put up with anthropologists asking questions and taking photos.

Piers Gibbon